Praise for
# The Way of Tea and Justice

"If you have not already met Becca Stevens of Thistle Farms fame, it's time you had the pleasure, and here's your chance. Just look how she shares tea and happiness—isn't she wonderful?"

—James Norwood Pratt, America's tea sage, author of
*James Norwood Pratt's Tea Dictionary*

"Becca Stevens is a force of nature—both as a speaker and with her words on the page. Her message always gets right to the heart of the matter."

—John Prine, songwriter

"[Women served by Thistle Farms] would be dead by now if it weren't for a remarkable initiative by the Rev. Becca Stevens...to help women escape trafficking and prostitution."

—Nicholas Kristof, *New York Times*

"With her characteristic warmth, wisdom, and insight, Becca Stevens opens up the strange and fascinating world of tea, masterfully stitching together stories about mindfulness, justice, healing, and community. Few writers exhibit such a remarkable ability to bring faith to life in the very world we can see, touch, taste, smell, and feel. Every word of this delightful, instructive book tastes like sacrament."

—Rachel Held Evans, author, *A Year of Biblical Womanhood*

# The Way of Tea and Justice

# The Way of Tea and Justice

## and
## Justice

### Rescuing the World's Favorite
### Beverage from Its Violent History

## BECCA STEVENS

JERICHO
BOOKS

New York • Boston • Nashville

Scripture quotations are from the New Revised Standard Version Bible, copyright © 1989 by the National Council of the Churches of Christ in the United States of America. Used by permission. All rights reserved.

Jericho Books
Hachette Book Group
1290 Avenue of the Americas
New York, NY 10104

www.JerichoBooks.com

Printed in the United States of America

RRD-C

First Edition: November 2014
10 9 8 7 6 5 4 3 2 1

Jericho Books is an imprint of Hachette Book Group, Inc.
The Jericho Books name and logo are trademarks of
Hachette Book Group, Inc.

The Hachette Speakers Bureau provides a wide range of authors for speaking events. To find out more, go to www.HachetteSpeakersBureau.com or call (866) 376-6591.

The publisher is not responsible for websites (or their content) that are not owned by the publisher.

Library of Congress Cataloging-in-Publication Data

Stevens, Becca, 1963–
  The way of tea and justice : rescuing the world's favorite beverage from its violent history / Becca Stevens.
    pages cm
  ISBN 978-1-4555-1902-6 (hardback)—ISBN 978-1-4555-1903-3 (ebook)
1. Tea—Social aspects.  2. Tea trade.  3. Competition, Unfair.  4. Social justice.  I. Title.
  GT2905.S85 2014
  394.1'5—dc23

2014011062

This book is dedicated to my sons in gratitude for all the truth they have taught me. These words are a prayer that the way of tea can offer you a place to center yourselves in the craziness of this life. I love you, Levi, Caney, and Moses. —Mom

This book is also offered in memory of Katie Stevens Garrett and Lisa Granoien Froeb.

# THE WAY OF TEA

*Tea is an invitation to take refuge*
*from the violence and vulnerability*
*poured out by the world.*
*She shelters us in leaves*
*steeped to soothe souls*
*with warm kisses.*
*Her aroma cradles us in*
*timeless dreams.*

*She is the ancient of days,*
*born by the tree of life.*
*She dined with Eve as the first sun set.*
*She is the harbinger of truth*
*whose hand-picked leaves*
*teach us how injustice is fed*
*on the bosom of poverty.*

*She is wisdom that incites*
*revolution and draws*
*enemies to treaties.*
*She has been worshiped*
*in rites that have bound and*
*freed generations.*

*She is universal,*
*born from a single leaf.*
*Her haloed cup is a sanctuary*
*for our thirst that longs*
*to love tenderly*
*with revived hearts.*

—Becca Stevens

# Contents

Contents

# Acknowledgments

I am so grateful to the team of capable volunteers and staff, including Dave Powell, Leigh Fitts, Orion Builders, Rob Barrick, Desmond and Curtis Child, Marcus Hummon, Marlei Olson, Tim Fudge, Courtney Johnson, Carlana Harwell, Peggy Napier, Yaara Yemin, Fiona Prine, Michael Kelsh, Al Strayhorn, Don Welch, Holli Anglin, Tammy Martin, Tonya Sneed, Joan Mayfield, Penny Hall, Sheri Brown, Gwen Cockrill, Katrina Robertson, Shana Goodwin, Chelle Waller, Rita Childs, Sidney Jordan, Anika Rogers, Julie Thames, Phil Nelson, Holly Dobberpuhl, Catherine Snell, Tom Robinson, James Worsham, Ali Harnell, Rolanda Johnson, Julie Cantrell, Jim Kensler, Gaile Owens, Tasha King, Terry Mitchell, Carolyn Snell, Kathy Nelson, Jennifer Clinger, Ronza Williams, Arleatha Walton, Tara Armistead, Tracy Warfield, Dorris Walker, Leticia Smith, Latisha Burns, Carole Hagan, Beth Preston, and Deb Markland. I am grateful to the entire board and staff at Thistle Farms and my fellow executive director, Cary Rayson. I am eternally grateful for the leadership of Dr. Sandy Stahl, who leads the board, and Dick Lodge, who has kept us legal for more than ten years. I am so proud of the whole staff and all the volunteers.

*Acknowledgments*

There were hundreds of volunteers led by Stacye Wilson, Susan Sluser, and Christy Beesley. I am always grateful to the community of St. Augustine's under the leadership of Mary Murphy and the community that gives so much in love. The staff of St. Augustine's, including Peggy McMurray, Brenda Beckham, Andrew Suitter, Chris Roberts, Lissa Smith, Toni Rogers, Scott Owings, and many more, provides the background laughter to all the work. I am grateful to Wendy Grisham and the whole team at Jericho, who let me write another book. I love all y'all. Thank you so, so much.

# The Way of
# Tea and Justice

# A BRIEF INTRODUCTION
# TO THE WORLD OF TEA

FIRST, AN EXPLANATION OF the recipes used at the beginning of each chapter: Acquiring all the ingredients to blend your own tea isn't easy but is well worth the effort. The blends and brands highlighted are well-known recipes offered by connoisseurs and pilgrims who have traveled far and wide to learn about taste and healing properties. They come from a variety of suppliers who specialize in a range of teas. Some of the teas highlighted are specifically selected because of their commitment not only to taste but also to the justice offered in the leaves to the people and land that grow them. You can find most of these blends at the places listed in this book and in books such as *Book of Tea, James Norwood Pratt's Tea Dictionary,* and *Taking Tea.* A wealth of information and recipes is also available online.

My hope is that you find blends that leave a good taste in your mouth, mind, and soul as you're led down an old and grounded spiritual path. Always look for teas that do not harm the people picking or packing them. Sometimes doing this requires researching beyond the fair-trade label

1

and into the harvesters' stories. Some teas listed are herbal tinctures and do not contain actual tea plants.

Even though there is just one plant known as tea, factors such as processing, geography, and rainfall combine into making a countless variety of teas that have different flavors, textures, colors, and aromas. Most tea experts divide these into eight major categories—black, green, white, oolong, pu-erh, herbal, yerba maté, and bush tea[1]—as well as a plethora of subcategories. These basic teas are like the Eightfold Path of Buddhism, which provides a strong foundation on which to build all the other categories of tea. Just as with keys on a piano, there are only eight notes in one octave, but once sharps, flats, ascending and descending order, timing, and creativity are added in, endless melodies emerge.

Throughout this book, I've included recommendations on how, where, and to whom to serve tea, because your *intention* as you serve is essential in the way of tea. How the plants are grown, how the water is boiled, how the serving cup is handled, and whom you share the beverage with can transform a plain black tea into a luxurious treat and a means for promoting justice across the world. Without concern for the tea or the way it is manufactured, an afternoon cup of expensive first-blush tea from an exotic region can leave you with a bitter taste in your mouth that is still parched for justice.

The idea for starting a teahouse called the Thistle Stop Café arose out of my work for Thistle Farms, a not-for-profit women's social enterprise based in Nashville, Tennessee, that employs fifty women. The organization began in 2001 as part of a program of residential communities called Magdalene that stand in solidarity with women who have survived lives of trafficking, addiction, and prostitution. I'd founded Thistle Farms because while we were helping women survive, they were unable to find work due to their criminal histories, addiction, and trauma. When we began, we were simply an all-natural bath and body care company with "Love Heals" as our tagline. We wanted the company to be run by the women, for the healing of the women, and to have a product that could engage us in the wider culture to discuss the myths and truths about why women walk the streets and what it takes to welcome those same women back home.

Over the past fifteen years, we built up a business generating more than $1 million annually, yet we still have a long waiting list of women looking for meaningful employment, which is critical to their economic independence and healing. Adding a new café could provide jobs and the opportunity for women to serve the thousands of visitors who come to Thistle Farms every year to see this community in action. In initial ideas for the café, I knew tea would need to play a central role to further the ambiance and story.

As if on cue, my friend Fiona, a native of Ireland, called to share some of her knowledge and love of tea. As I shared the new vision for the café, Fiona affirmed that tea could become central to our venture into justice. She offered to host a tea party at her home so we could begin to learn the way of tea. I gathered with eight others from the community of Thistle Farms around her dining room table. We were awestruck by the care for detail: three-layer serving dishes, tiny sandwiches, scones with real cream, and proper china teacups. I was mesmerized by the way tea set the mood of the table and the generosity expressed in the serving. By the time we left her house, everyone was ready to host a tea party at Thistle Farms. Especially me.

More than anything, I craved the relaxation and rest that drinking tea could bring to my life and to the community. Thistle Farms is no small enterprise. We manufacture and ship almost half a million products around the globe each year. In addition, we've helped launch more than twenty sister programs across the country. While our community is a refuge, it's also a place where dozens of employees and volunteers scurry around with various responsibilities and tasks. Some days it feels like a vortex of chaos. We don't have a set hierarchical structure, so decisions are made by casual consensus. This is a beautiful model in principle, but in practice it can be a bit confusing and frustrating. The frustration is compounded by the fact that on any given day in the life of a recovering woman, any employee may relapse.

Maybe it's this chaos that fueled the fantasy that groups of people, myself included, could gather in a peaceful space and sip tea. Perhaps I had allowed tea to woo me into believing that it could bring peace to work each day. I didn't calculate just how much *more* daily work would be required in opening the new café.

\*     \*     \*

We decided to launch Thistle Stop Café in January 2013. When we first began dreaming, we had no idea about the complex the world of café design, health codes, and operational needs we were entering into. In the beginning, the idea was simple: Whatever we served would be as good for the earth as it is for our bodies, in keeping with the mission of Thistle Farms products. We'd offer simple baked goods and salads, and become a welcoming kind of teahouse.

From the moment we began to talk about the café, there was a lot of interest from the women at Thistle Farms to work there. They loved the idea of waitressing and designing the uniforms they wanted to wear. A couple of the employees wanted to wear T-shirts and jeans while there were others who suggested purple aprons and black skirts. I made no comment since the beauty is that they were envisioning a future they were literally going to be draped in. Each woman wrote her own story and shared it for this book. The women are eloquent and have reminded me that they didn't always imagine a future for themselves. All of the stories are similar to countless stories you hear from other women who work at Thistle Farms: There was physical and sexual abuse at a very young age, drugs and sex came on its heels, and a downward spiral was perpetuated by an unjust penal system and no access to wealth. Sometimes when I sip tea with one of the employees and listen to her story, I can't help but let my mind wonder what the woman would be doing if she had not experienced abuse and gripping poverty. But I usually stop myself as the thought rises. Even in my own life with my history of abuse I don't have that thought anymore. Now it's about taking the stories of brokenness and weaving them together to form a tapestry of hope for others. As the journey to the café began, we started thinking about what was the most basic thing we would need to open it. We wanted to foster the fellowship and healing tea enables, and we wanted to increase the demand for tea grown by women earning good wages. The first thing we needed: teacups.

We began by collecting old teacups from around the world as a way to engage people in the vision of the café. We asked donors to share the story of their cups. This became a signature for us as we embraced the motto "A story in every cup." These stories carried us back a hundred years into rich histories, politics, personal victories, and intimate journeys. One of my favorites is a broken cup sent by the daughter of a man who was a refugee from the Bosnian war during the 1990s. She described the heroic nature of survival and how broken things can still be beautiful. We cataloged her story and took a picture of the cup and the other thousand cups that were donated over the next year. Every detail of the café—from the teacups, to the tea, to the women who serve our customers—all carry a powerful story.

What we didn't know when we launched was the power that came with the word "tea." It threw open the doors of an unfamiliar, ancient, complex, and nuanced world. Not everyone who heard about our idea to open a café responded well to the idea of serving tea. One person complained that the tea was "colonial" and was "oppressive" to women. Another argued that we didn't know how to serve a proper tea or about the complexity of tea, and didn't need to try and get into the business. Tea turned out to be more powerful than we had anticipated. Because the reaction was strong, it confirmed for us that tea would be a vehicle for healing all of us. I could already imagine tasting thistle tea with a hint of lavender.

This is the story of the journey that the Thistle Farms community has been on and how we've been changed through the way of tea. This is not a full history of tea or a complete guide to becoming a connoisseur but insights into what we learned from tea and how it became a faithful companion. Along this road, we discovered the myth of fair trade in the tea market, the longing for justice among pickers and growers, and the desire to find teas that we could serve that were rooted in truth. Along the way, tea has provided a colorful lens through which we can contemplate theology and the heavens.

Tea isn't a quick fix but a long journey into hope. My hope is that this book, like a steaming cup of your favorite blend, will bring you moments of peace and sanity in this crazy world.

## Chapter One

# READING TEA LEAVES

## A Black Kenyan Justice Tea

I stumbled upon Ajiri, a black tea from Kenya, while visiting the Smithsonian African Museum in Washington, DC. Drawn to the elegant artisan boxes depicting scenes made from tiny paper cut-outs, I soon learned that the manufacturer creates employment for the people of western Kenya. All profits are used to educate orphans in the community. We selected to use this award-winning specialty tea in our café for its social justice aftertaste.

To enjoy: Fill a small tea ball halfway with the loose leaves.

Steep this tea, like most black teas, in hot water for 3 minutes.

After steeping, a bit of lemon juice brings out the best flavors.

The tea is even more delicious knowing the goal of the company is to care for the most vulnerable members of the community.

At Thistle Stop Café, we serve Ajiri in to-go boxes as well as offer the loose-leaf tea. In many teahouses, it is unacceptable to give someone a tea bag and a cup of hot water. Tea is served properly in pots with a container for the loose leaves, which is a slower process than offering a hot cup with a tea bag. But it is that that reminds us to slow down and savor each sip.

THE FIRST TIME I looked into the bottom of a teacup to study the leaves, I saw my reflection. My hair was frizzed at the ends and looked like a dried-out halo. A friend and I were finishing up lunch when I noticed loose green tea leaves floating at the bottom of my cup. On a whim, I told him that I could read the leaves.

The conversation had been swirling around tea and the new idea of opening a café as part of Thistle Farms.

"Can you really read tea leaves?" my friend asked. As I looked into the cup and saw my ragged and shadowed halo of hair, I answered, "I guess I can."

The way of tea teaches us that if we pause and take the time to look closely enough, it is possible that all of us can find ourselves in a good cup of tea. A single leaf of tea is enough to examine the whole universe. Tea offers us contemplation that is so rich and old, if we had eyes to see, time to taste, and a thirst for its truth, we could travel to the ends of the earth and plumb the depths of our hearts. The way of tea can lead us to visit old-growth forests in China, through rituals more than two thousand years old and into a space of meditation where we remember all hearts are made of flesh.

The day I saw my reflection glistening in the golden brew of a teacup, I took it as a sign. By the end of the lunch I knew I wanted to learn everything I could about the way of tea before the café opened. This included developing a palate for tea, learning about the sources of tea, and understanding the issues of justice in the growing and trading of tea, as well as understanding the role tea could play in helping guide our movement of helping women find healing. Soon enough, tea had taken a hold of me, reminded me of my past, and stirred a longing for justice.

My mom was my first guide on the way of tea. She lived by intuition and fortitude. She taught me that when it comes to a spiritual journey, it's better to lead by the heart and not follow the well-worn path. When we make our own discoveries, there's an organic element of surprise that signifies the spirit is leading us. It's a harder path, but it also makes things your own. My mother used to fix tea when I was a child. She worked long, exhausting days running a community center and mothering five kids as a single parent. I remember every evening after the supper dishes were washed; she made a cup of inexpensive Lipton tea. After steeping the tea bag for a few minutes, she wrapped the tea bag's string around a spoon to squeeze out the richer, blacker droplets. She stored the used tea bag in the spoon beside the sink so she could make a second cup later.

Tea was my mom's faithful companion throughout her life. Tea carried her through saying good-bye to her husband at the age of thirty-five, through seeing all of her children grow up and out of the house, and through her terminal illness that took her life at the age of sixty-three. Many of my mom's habits and beliefs have helped form my path. Since she was an avid tea drinker, it only made sense that tea would eventually make its way into the heart of my spiritual journey. When I think of her today, I can still picture her holding the teacup with a thistle pattern from her tea set close to her chest like a prayer.

Tea warmed my mother's heart, mind, and body, just as it has mine. Like her, I find comfort in hearing the whistle of the kettle in the evening and holding the cup close to my body. Like her, I still wrap the string around the bag and spoon. When I drink my tea and save the tea bag to use again, I can imagine she, too, felt the allure of peace and beauty that drew her in as much as the flavor of the drink.

My mother rarely got to drink loose-leaf tea. Almost all her evenings were spent using tea bags that are filled with "tea dust," the discarded bits and pieces of tea after producers have collected the loose-leaf tea. What was in the cup was less important than what the tea offered. It offered freedom in time and space to feel comfort and to let her mind wander. Like her, drinking tea gives me freedom to dream beautiful and idealistic thoughts.

Unlike her, I long to have cups of tea filled not with tea bags but with loose leaves swirling as they soak. Loose-leaf tea dances and comes to life in hot water, offering a healing delight to once-plain liquid. We are restored by the tea's gifts, even after the cup is drained and we are left with limp leaves sitting at the bottom. As I began to pay attention to the art of tea, I loved the idea that perhaps there were signs even at the bottom of an old teacup. It was the leaves that first drew me into learning what tea was willing to teach.

Loose tea drew me in because of its similarities to the living plant and because it holds more of the goodness of the original plant than the tea dust in bags. I hoped staring into the leaves could spell out the next steps of my dream to offer justice to women who have survived trafficking, prostitution, and addiction. A connection existed between the tea and the women I longed to empower, but I wasn't sure how to find the answer to how they were related. I longed for instant insight into what I needed to do. But perhaps the first step of insight is recognizing how little we know.

Maybe ignorance is a gift. Lack of knowledge at the beginning of a journey can offer us courage to start new ventures. If I'd known how difficult it was going to be to launch Thistle Farms or the café, I may have never taken the first step. If any of the team at Thistle Farms had realized how expensive it would be or how much of our hearts we needed to pour into this dream, we may have just kept talking about tea leaves over lunch. The blissful ignorance of inspiration made me think, "Let's open a beautiful café with tea and serve a million cups to friends and strangers, and start a new tea revolution to help end trafficking. How hard can it be?"

As a movement, Thistle Farms was growing at an exponential rate and shipping products to more than three hundred stores around the country. If we wanted to continue to grow, we needed to step into our role as a welcoming site for people who wanted to join in the conversation and learn about human trafficking and how they could help be a part of women finding their freedom. The Thistle Stop Café could serve as a hub for people to have conversations, gain sanctuary, and introduce themselves to our community.

Trafficking is a direct result of silence and ignorance by communities. It is rooted in the desire to keep the sickness of addiction and child abuse secret. The more light we can shed on the issues and the more we can help educate the population, the safer our whole community will be. The cafe would provide pastors and friends a place to bring folks who were abused and scared to speak their truth. We would offer the business community a place for meetings where women are held in high esteem. We would even begin to hold up the women's stories as more than survivor stories but ones that ground us all in the truth that love can change the way we treat one another in this world.

In all of our lives, blissful ignorance keeps us dreaming and moving forward. We forget that *living* a dream is much harder than talking about a dream. When we get ready to climb the mountain, we have no idea the storms we will face on the way. We can't imagine the sounds at night that will keep us awake with fear. Excitement blinds us to the countless hours of hard work required before inspiration becomes reality. The lack of knowledge at the beginning is a sacred space. If we embrace it, we can learn to thrive in that thick space of time between inspiration and actuality.

This sacred space is where we gain the knowledge we need to go further. It is a hard and rocky ground that calls us into sleepless nights and anxious moments. Sometimes that space is short; other times it can last a lifetime. Usually it is the exact amount of time we need to learn and gain the resources to carry out the venture. The space between now and then is the holy path of hard work. I am used to that space being longer and harder than I imagined, but I still wish for magical insight to come and speed things up.

This space between the dream and actuality is usually more grueling than we plan for at Thistle Farms. Opening up the first residential home within our community took two years. Another two years was required to get our social enterprise off the ground. Six years in, we built our first house from the ground up. The years ticked by in uneven increments. Along the way, wisdom led us to follow more dreams. Looking back, I needed every minute.

The ratio of dream to reality is in direct proportion to sweat equity and time. When my husband of twenty-five years, Grammy-winning songwriter Marcus Hummon, creates a cantata, the melody in his head doesn't come to fruition right away. First he plays with the idea for hours, modifying and repeating the tune. Then he adds cello and background sounds to truly appreciate the beauty of the initial dream. Working hard on the piece and spending the time charting and recording it hones the original melody, gives time to edit lyrics, and allows the gift of bringing thoughts to life. When a friend of mine who is a landscape architect talks about developing a piece of land, she has to begin with a blank piece of paper and sit on the actual land alone to let it speak to her. That time and space is invaluable to her so that she doesn't impose herself on the land but lets the land thrive through her work. If she went in knowing what she wanted to design, she would miss the insight the land itself can offer.

The insight we need comes from long contemplation, conversation, and dogged determination. Insight, like a precipice, requires one to climb to the top of a mountain to breathe in the view. We have to endure those long nights and storms to get to the place where the view is even possible. Insight doesn't come to us just because we wish we had it. We can read a passage of Scripture for years before it comes to life. We can round the same bend in the woods for seasons until one day we finally see the Eden we have been walking through. Just because I wanted to see something beautiful and deep in the bottom of my tea didn't mean I would.

Insight comes from inspired work in which we learn from both our successes and our failures. Insight doesn't come from wishing or imagining. If we did have the answers spelled out for us before we began our journey, there would be no reason to take the journey. We'd miss out on the sense of "Eureka" or the lessons we could have learned. Not knowing what lies ahead is no reason not to start walking. When we find ourselves afraid of failure or worrying about success, the best thing to do is just keep our heads down and take another step forward. If we just stay where we are, we will never get anywhere. I had no clue what I was looking for staring into the cup, but it was enough just to be looking. Insights are gained by hard lessons that unfold during journeys of new understanding and ventures like tea and justice. It seems crazy sometimes to think that any of us can try to change the world by our small inspirations of justice, but it is crazier to think that the world will change if we never try.

The art of reading tea leaves is known as tasseography, a kind of fortune-telling that interprets patterns. The practice is rooted in a desire to understand ourselves and make sense of the world. Tasseography was popularized as a kind of parlor game and is seen as a tool for tapping into the subconscious by applying insight and meaning to pattern recognition. But like any kind of mystical endeavor, reading tea leaves loses something in translation when we read the instruction guide.

A great description of reading leaves can be found in the book *Taking Tea*.[2] The authors claim some of the first tea readers were the Scottish, who could read the leaves "like a gypsy." These readers would get up early in the morning because reading the breakfast tea leaves determined the mood of the day. If it was going to be unlucky, the person should just get back in bed.

Reading tea requires loose tea poured unstrained into cups. After everyone finishes their tea, they offer silent wishes like the thoughts before you blow out birthday candles or throw a coin into a fountain. The reader of the leaves takes the cup and swirls it three times clockwise. Then the reader inverts the cup on the saucer until the last drip of tea runs off. At that moment, the reader turns the cup upright again; the leaves stick to the bottom. The tea reader then searches for shapes in the leaves, such as birds, animals, numbers, or outlines of maps that might allude to the future of the drinker.

I stared at the bottom of my favorite mug searching for these magical, elusive images. I even tried blurring my eyes to see the leaves as I did for those magic three-dimensional images that became popular in the 1990s. The trick was to stare deep enough into the artwork until the blurry dots revealed the hidden three-dimensional image. Staring into the bottom of my favorite white mug, I allowed my eyes to blur and refocus, waiting patiently for everything to become clear. At first, I thought I might be looking at Chinese characters, but since I cannot read Chinese, I figured I was probably still staring into a pile of wilted leaves. Then I shifted my focus to the negative space to see if the lighter areas had something to reveal.

The leaves are not full of insight and truth just because I want them to be. Though I long for vision to be presented like a floral bouquet, beautiful and neat, it rarely appears as easily or readily. In my own life, insights come quickly only in rare moments such as a low-flying hawk casting a shadow over a wild thistle nearby. In those beautiful times insight rises like a new thought out of a morning mist. But far and away I mostly gain insight from rearview mirrors that reflect the gift of making my way by hard work and the discernment of sweat and tears.

In the ensuing weeks, what struck me was how I continued to picture tea leaves in my mind's eye. I could see tea leaves in a bundle of owl feathers I spotted on a forest path. Tea leaves emerged in late-afternoon storm clouds. Tea-leaf shapes appeared in melting ice cubes in my glass. Finally it dawned on me that I needed actually to see the leaves themselves and quit trying to imagine something else. I needed to see what was before me. Often, when we step into something new, we don't recognize that what we need next is right before us.

The insight that I needed literally came from reading the story of actual tea leaves. Leaves strewn on a saucer come from somewhere and were picked by someone. They have earned the honor of being the oldest cultivated plant on record. These leaves of wisdom are rooted back before time was recorded, set firmly in creation. It is not enough to dump them onto a saucer and see if they fall in a way that spells out something magical. Instead, these leaves are a launching pad for a spiritual path. Staring at the leaves when I began dreaming of a café, I got the message that it was time to dive into this cup, study the books, and learn how to read all that the leaves had to teach.

## Knowing the Leaves

To make beautiful tea, you have to know the leaves. There are close to three thousand leaf varieties with a myriad of blending possibilities. Green tea leaves are the most healing types. After green tea leaves are picked, they are left in the sun for a couple of hours and then are pan fired. Then the leaves are rolled and put back into the fire again. Once this is done, people pick out any remaining stems, and then the tea is bagged. To make black tea, the green leaves of a tea plant are left in the sun for a whole day. After about twelve hours, the leaves are turned. Black tea is not technically fermented, but cured. Curing allows black tea to brew darker and a bit more bitter once it is put into water.

The story that the tea leaves tell has filled books that trace the entire history of civilization and cover the spectrum of humanity including revolution, oppression, ritual, and culture. The story of tea is one of romance, renewal, and reflection. The lessons of tea unfold not just in a huge complicated historical story but also in sweet personal memories that live in our hearts. We should approach tea with great reverence for the million lessons it can teach us along the way. In the small rituals of wrapping tea bag strings around a spoon or staring into the bottom of a cup, the story of tea comes alive.

I drink tea as I write this manuscript. I drink it while I research, interview people, and pray. I am not even sure where it is leading. I don't know yet if the café will stay a dream or open. I wait and watch to see who will share their cup with the community of Thistle Farms. When you drink enough tea, you can start to feel it take root and change your composition. You lose your taste for coffee, and you long to hold the warmth of the teacup in your hands. Tea will lure you like a young lover, calling you with the oldest siren song to come and drink from this cup that offers insight and new life. I want to drink more and get to the root of where it comes from and see where it leads. I want to find out how justice tastes on the backs of the oldest leaves that, like the women of Thistle Farms, have survived so much injustice. But I want us all to drink tea with our eyes wide open, not lured by fancy packaging that blindsides us and begs us to judge the book by the cover. The same humble tea can be dressed up like it's going to afternoon tea at Buckingham

Palace or preparing for meditation in a Tibetan monastery. Tea can be Zen, or organic, or girly, or colonial. It can be as tempting as an apple in a wild garden—that is part of its romance. My hope is to get through the packaging and find how justice can be pursued in the buying and selling of tea and how all of us can share a cup and celebrate freedom.

Even after reading countless books and studying the ancient practices, I still can't read leaves except to recognize that they call me to pay attention. Instead, what I've learned by searching for hidden patterns in wet tea leaves is that opportunities are ever before us. When we keep our eyes open, there's no telling what image may emerge. As we begin to move forward to lay hold of those visions and dreams, we will encounter setbacks, detours, disappointments, and fears. But if we push forward in reverence and humility, we may uncover a future better than we ever could have imagined. Tea can help us get there. It allows us to see something holy and romantic in simply pouring a cup of hot water over a bag and sipping in the gifts of creation. Through a cup of tea, the whole world can open up.

*Chapter Two*

# DREAMING A CUP
# OF TEA

## A Rwandan Black Tea

Rwanda was estimated to produce almost one quarter of the fair-trade tea imported into the United States in 2012. Drinking teas that are part of the Rainforest Alliance programs and the Ethical Tea Partnership, both organizations in Rwanda committed to working with tea growers, ensures ecologically sensitive land use as well as good working conditions and fair treatment for workers. Rwandan black tea can be blended with other herbs that make it even more delicious, uplifting, and hopeful.

To make an uplifting tea for winter, use St. John's wort for a healthy and tasty combination with a kick of positivity.

Boil water in a kettle.

Mix 2 tablespoons Rwandan black tea with 1 tablespoon St. John's wort. Place the mixture into a loose-leaf holder inside a teapot and let steep 3 minutes.

Enjoy with a friend, and remind one another of the beautiful landscapes of the world that are healing from wars and keeping hope alive.

SMALL TEA STAINS ON the pages of my well-read tea books look like breadcrumbs on a path toward the insight I long for. I keep sipping tea and flipping pages and finding myself heading down a windy path that leaves me in awe. Sipping tea invites us to imagine the plant's origins, soil, roots, and journey to the cup. Drinking tea opens an old, old story that is worth knowing. Tracing the roots of tea back to the beginning gives tea a richer flavor and helps us figure out how we went astray so that we can reclaim the goodness of the plant and get back on course. Like humanity, tea begins with original grace in a place called Eden where there was nothing to distinguish a weed from a flower.

In *The Story of Tea*, Mary Lou and Robert J. Heiss give a wonderful description of how the first wild tea plants originated from the Yunnan region in China known as the Seven Tea Mountains. Tea explorers like them have written about tea plants there that rise sixty feet into the air and are over a thousand years old. These plants in the forest of China are the Eve in the mother line of tea plants, and they have witnessed the spinning of the earth around the sun hundreds of times over. Humanity's life span is fleeting compared to those old Chinese plants.

While native varieties are found in Assam, India, and South China, they are part of the same botanical classification, and horticulturists have concluded that there is only one species called tea in the world. This one species of tea plant, the *Camellia sinensis*, means that all the tea we drink, whether from India, South America, or China, shares a common heritage and is related. Thus tea becomes a beautiful symbol of the theological truth that we are all connected, and although each kind of processed tea has different effects and flavors, it's like love: It all comes from the same source but can be expressed a thousand ways. Not only are we drinking something beautiful, we are sipping something universal both in its roots and its application. Tea is the tie that binds us, and the tea we drink invites us to share a common heritage with the whole world. By finding and drinking teas from anywhere in the world that are grown and picked with justice as a core value of tea owners and growers, we are sharing a cup with a world that still thirsts to reclaim our past for a more equitable future. When we drink tea, we are connected to every other tea drinker in the world by the virtue of the common plant and the global trade. A woman who has taken off her burka in the safety of a friend's parlor in Saudi Arabia is having a common experience of fellowship to that of a man walking into the famous London department store Harrod's for an afternoon tea. A new mom leaning over a small stove heating water in rural Kenya is sharing the anticipation that a woman in Tokyo feels in a high-rise downtown after a long day of work. Tea calls us to her altar and doesn't discriminate or judge. It is truly a holy drink throughout the world. No other drink besides water carries such a claim or connects us so literally.

The first stories of tea being cultivated date back more

than thirty-five hundred years to an emperor harvesting the first of what we associate now as green tea. A thousand years later, the curing process would develop, and black tea would be processed. Tea's history is central to the history of the Eastern world. By the Shang dynasty, in the eleventh century BCE, tea was beginning to be used for medicinal purposes. Seven hundred years later, in the Zhou dynasty, around the third century BCE, people began to boil the leaves for consumption. About the time that Jesus walked through Galilee, the first tea gardens were being cultivated in Sichuan Province. The journey of tea continued to be refined for another two thousand years in its planting, processing, and serving.

The historical journey of tea often parallels the history of trade as well as the struggle for power and wealth. In the sixth century of the modern era, leaves were first steamed and made into hard tea cakes that could be transported. This shift opened up new trade possibilities and allowed for the addition of spices into the tea because the cakes preserved the tea. It also meant that tea became a currency that could be traded. Monks on pilgrimages first carried tea from the forests of China into Japan, and tea became one of the currencies used throughout Mongolia, across central Asia, and into Afghanistan, Kashmir, and Tibet. Along with silk and cotton, tea became a major currency of trade, and routes were created to support its rich economic benefits. Tea was a powerful commodity, and by the twelfth century other industries like porcelain making and transportation grew up around it. By the seventeenth century, Portuguese and Dutch traders were transporting tea to England in the growing import sector of the economy. The trading of tea would lead to smuggling, death, wars, treaties, and enslavement.

In *A Brief History of Tea* by Roy Moxham there are stories about the impact of importing tea into England in the mid-eighteenth century. There is one story that details how tea smugglers captured two law enforcement officers, tortured them, and buried one alive. When the gang of tea smugglers was finally captured, "they were to be hanged, and then—a punishment hugely feared—to be chained and left hanging in the open as a warning." The story illustrates the power beyond the drink and the desire to control its trading. Smuggling, burying people alive, and hanging as punishment are testimony to the importance of tea and its ability to influence global trading practices and laws as well as incite the mistreatment of humans.

Tea led to the battle cry for the Revolutionary War in the United States and instigated the Opium Wars in China. Through the journey of tea we can trace how international trade dramatically changed after the Opium Wars and how the secrets of processing tea were stolen and exported throughout the world. These events will be explored later in the book, but it is important to note here that looking at tea's past can illuminate deeper truths about history. Tea provides a window through which we can view a global history.

One of the most fascinating paragraphs in tea's long history is how the dowry of Princess Catherine of Portugal for King Charles II of England contained a chest of tea and the gift of Bombay (Mumbai), both of which led to the growth of what was arguably the most powerful corporation the world has known, the East India Trading Company. Charles II gave this company power to launch its own ships of war and to provide "for ever hereafter...the whole entire and only trade and traffick...to and from the said East Indies."[3] The establishment of the tea estates in India was a source of unimaginable oppression and untold wealth for the British colonies of India and Ceylon (now Sri Lanka). The growing of tea requires cheap labor, and the colonization of India and countries in Africa provided it through exploited labor. In the late nineteenth century, the conditions for transporting labor from remote farming villages to the tea estates were abysmal, resulting in some mortality rates as high as 50 percent due to cholera, malaria, and malnourishment.[4]

The conditions on the tea estates in India into the twentieth century include stories of rapes, beatings, and shootings of the workforce by estate owners and managers. There are reports from tea planters in the early twentieth century that "a manager may assault a laborer, insult him, and take girl after girl from the lines as his mistress, yet there will be none to dispute his action or authority."[5]

Throughout its history, tea has been not only witness to war and treaties but companion on many of the great explorations of the last five hundred years. There are great stories and examples of how tea helped warm weary hearts and minds as Europeans took to the seas to find new countries to conquer and unseen tundra upon which to sink their flags. Tea was used to keep men warm aboard the *Endurance* in 1914 when the crew found themselves stranded on the icebergs off Antarctica. The *Endurance* hit ice before it reached Antarctica and in the face of almost certain death, the men continued the tea ritual. There are great stories of how Ernest Shackleton, the captain, brought tea to men on sledges as they were hunting seals to keep them alive during the winter. During their eighteen months on ice, you can imagine what the men must have felt seeing the supplies of tea dwindle. Shackleton's own account describes how they began to drink the stuffing from their boots like tea.

Tea was also there in World War II in England to sustain people. The historian A. A. Thompson wrote in 1942, "They talk about Hitler's secret weapon, but what about England's secret weapon—tea. That's what keeps us going and that's what's going to carry us through."[6] Tea was privy to war room conversations and a friend to the fighting men. The government, to safeguard tea, took control of all stocks at the war's outset. In 1940, after blockades prevented ships from getting through, tea was rationed to 2 ounces per person per week, but men in the armed forces received extra. Tea was such a morale booster that it was even sent in Red Cross parcels to British prisoners of war.

Tea was integral in the struggle for Indian independence. The tea estates that were a crucial part of manufacturing wealth to England had long been able to isolate the workforce and treat laborers as if they were indentured servants. The luxurious tea coming from Assam, India, continued to be an oppressive tool used by England to extract high profits and oppress workers. Mohandas Gandhi's independence movement in India helped improve the rights of the tea workers and connect them to the National Congress. Tea became a tool Gandhi used against those who wanted to use the leaves to enslave people. He helped to organize workers and find alternatives to tea grown on huge estates, and he finally served tea to the British who would oppress the Indian people as a demonstration of his theology. In a beautiful scene in the movie *Gandhi*, his leadership team asks him not to serve tea. Through pouring the tea, he demonstrates the theology of ahimsa, the soul force of love that seeks to cause no pain and that can change all our hearts and minds. While wages and treatment of tea workers have vastly improved, it doesn't take much research to find stories of worker exploitation in every country with tea estates.[7]

Finally, in addition to being a window into history, economics, exploration, and oppression, tea was central to the formation of rituals and rejuvenation in the three great philosophy religions of Buddhism, Confucianism, and Taoism. The story of the development of the rituals of tea offers a glimpse into theology and a life of prayer. To this day, the beverage beckons us to join in the ritual of serving and drinking tea that teaches us about culture, history, and God. While history traces the harrowing path tea traveled and the oceans it crossed, the story I am drawn to first is that of the tea planters, pickers, and producers. The poverty experienced by most tea pickers throughout history is a bitter brew. Poverty preys on the most vulnerable members of society, in this case women and children, who historically have picked tea most. Their silent and unwritten story calls to people who savor tea and long for justice to better understand tea growing and production and to demand fairer practices for the world's tea harvesters.

Five years ago I stood in a field in the hills of Rwanda and had my first thoughts about wanting to understand the struggle for justice in the growing tea industry in the years since the 1994 genocide. Rwanda is known for importing tea to the States that is organic and fair trade. But when I first stood in the beautiful fields, which were being harvested by those who had survived the genocide, I couldn't help but compare the incredible beauty of the fields and the stories of the burden of poverty that some of the pickers shared. When you're in the fields you can't help but fall in love with the agrarian landscape outside of Kigali and feel a deep desire to understand more about what justice in growing and trading tea looks like. That was a long time ago, though, and I wasn't yet thinking that tea would become so prominent in my journey.

I met Nicholas Hitimana, the founding director of a cooperative called Ikirezi, and toured an organic farm where over four hundred women farmers partnered to grow lemongrass, germanium, and eucalyptus, to distill essential oils. They use the profits to build houses for one another and their surviving children. I was invited to sit in their kitchens, sip tea, and listen to their stories. There was a deep connection between the stories of the sexual violence they encountered and those I hear weekly from the women in the Thistle Farms community. Their stories of survival were similarly heroic, and their ability to inspire hope in others was miraculous.

One woman told of crouching in waist-deep wet fields while fellow citizens were slaughtering her neighbors and family during the Rwandan genocide. Another woman's arm had been amputated in the genocide. Despite the loss and pain, she chose to forgive and kept farming. Others were more hesitant to talk, and some didn't want to speak of the genocide at all. When they talked about their families, they simply said "before 1994"—the year of the genocide—and spoke of the children they had then and now. Listening to what was spoken and left unspoken, I could feel a heavy weight pressing on my chest. I felt the guilt and grief we all bear from the knowledge that humanity is capable of such horror. Their stories followed me home and sit with me as I sip rich Rwandan black tea, reminded of the untold history of the people who cultivated it.

As I picture the women I met, I taste richness in this black tea that mirrors some of the richest soil on earth. I can see them standing in a field of four-foot-high bushes during twelve-hour shifts, wearing colorful headscarves, patterned dresses, and flip-flops. I wonder how they just keep picking and picking to fill baskets attached to their thin bodies. I recently asked Nicholas if he thought that the tea that he and I were drinking on his recent trip to Nashville could link us closer to the women of Rwanda. He explained the importance of direct trade in the business of social enterprise justice. Direct trade simply means that products move in a direct path from the producer to the consumer. The more direct the path, the higher the producer is valued in the economic equation. He was passionate about our ability, as consumers of essential oils and teas from Rwanda, to shift the winds of trade in the women's favor through wise purchasing practices.

My time in Rwanda reminds me that we are all connected. We are connected just like all the tea plants come from the same roots. The women who grow and pick the leaves are connected to the consumers. The women who will serve this tea at the Thistle Stop Café will forever be connected to the growers of this tea. If we can remind ourselves of the connection, we can build a world of fairer-traded tea.

I continue to look into the history of tea and I am struck by the patterns of human institutions that create poverty and yoke it to women. As I sipped my tea from a justice-minded farm in Rwanda, which is still in the minority of how most tea is plucked and processed, I could almost taste the hope that arises when work is done in a spirit of fairness and community.

Tea leaves from Rwanda that once might have held rich flavor lose their taste if we don't pay attention to the poverty of women who spend their lives in the hills of Kigali picking them. Our palates need to be cultivated to the point that we can savor the place of the tea producers in the value chain of trade and economics. When we thirst for justice tea as consumers, it will be there for us to drink. This means we need to purchase tea where farms are owned by participants, promote direct trade, and are organic companies that work to leverage economic market share and consumer awareness. The cooperatives emerging in Rwanda are meeting these criteria through the shared values and responsibility meted out through governing boards that don't profit from increased trade. Rwandan tea is a good reminder that what we consume can either free or oppress. Hearing the quiet taste calling for justice in every cup is critical to the healing of the world. It's not enough to drink tea. We must know how it is grown.

Before I could even imagine exactly what the café would look like, I was already dreaming of the women we would hire to serve the tea. I hoped that customers could feel that tea grown with justice and dignity and served by survivors tastes richer. I hoped that strangers who walked into the café thirsty for much more than a cup of tea would be bonded by the common idea that we all have a story and that is what brings us together. I wanted to hold as sacred the stories of the hired women, the tea producers, and the customers. The café would support real economic development for the individual working women by training them as baristas and cashiers, offering full-time living wages, and providing a healing community where there is sufficient time and space to gain economic independence and make restitution with courts, family, and self. The scars of childhood trauma carried by the employed women are older than the oldest tea trees in the seven-story mountains of China. The women have a history of injustice and oppression as deep and rooted as the tea itself. A deep connection exists between the story of the women of Thistle Farms and the tea they serve.

My prayer is that the women working in the café will heal as they serve. They will not "get over" the sexual violence they have experienced, but they will find roots that run deeper. They will keep serving tea until the past fades far enough into the background that a future comes into focus. This café will be part of their long journey of healing in the way of tea. They will see that the deep brutality they have borne on their backs was not in vain. Their suffering can be used to preach love as the most powerful force for social change. Because they survived and live in recovery, the beauty of their laughter comes from a place of gratitude and wholeness. Wisdom in living in recovery has changed them forever into courageous women whose dreams never die. Tea and Thistle Farms are bonded by their common history of survival, longevity, grace, and healing. The hope of women coming to the café whom I have not yet met is a reminder that tea will have a practical and economic side that will expand our reach. More than sweet thoughts, tea can become an economic powerhouse that transforms the history of communities. Tea can be a source of economic independence for women instead of a source of oppression. But like many good dreams, this one requires insight, forethought, and planning. We know we want the women in our community to make a living wage. We want to ensure everything we serve is as good for the earth as it is for the body. But we also need to establish the parameters of our economic bottom line and identify the underlying principles for managing this new venture.

It was time to establish specifically what those underlying principles would be so that they could be our guide for serving up a revolutionary tea while honoring the historical way of tea. Narrowing these principles down to four was one of my first goals to present to the committee that would help launch this new venture.

The first principle that needs to ground our community is hospitality. Hospitality is at the heart of the Benedictine rule, which helped form the spiritual practice of Magdalene and Thistle Farms.[8] The café will be welcoming to guests because we recognize the dignity of every person. Each visitor will be considered a member of the community of Thistle Farms during their visit. To live into this principle, we need to create a warm and kind place where people feel their spirits as well as their bodies fed and loved. This principle can be lived in simple details like fresh flowers on every table, a large guest book for input and comments, fragrant oils diffused throughout the café, enough staff and volunteers to bring the tea to each table and take a moment to listen to the journey of how guests made their way into this space.

*Chado*, which simply means "the way of tea" in Japanese, is the second principle guiding our café. Everything we do needs to reflect our desire to create harmony, cleanness, and tranquility. All the trappings of beauty are as temporal as the flowers, but in *chado*, we can offer guests a glimpse of love. The café is an outward and visible sign of the deeper meaning of healing. For folks to get the deeper meaning of what we are offering, they will need an open heart and a bit of reflection. We are taking an old universal practice and reminding people that the place of honor is the place of service for those who thirst.

Story is the third principle that will guide us. My hope is that the Thistle Stop Café will be a place to honor the individual stories of courage that give hope to the world. A story will be found in the tea (and coffee) we serve. The floor, the furniture, and the cabinets will all carry stories as well. Those who work in the café and those who wander in all have a story, and we want to make space for people to share their stories with one other without judgment in an atmosphere of acceptance and love. Sometimes the stories will be shared through chance meetings and long afternoon conversations. Other times we will make space to display a story found in music, writing, or poetry. And sometimes the story a visitor most needs to hear will be told through the artwork and sculptures found throughout the café. The Thistle Stop Café will be a place for humanity to bring and share their stories knowing they'll be heard.

The final essential principle is healing. Our tea will be all natural and served with respect for the gifts of creation that help our bodies, minds, and spirits. Community is a powerful agent of healing. By opening the doors, we are creating a space for the servers, the guests who come in, and the people who read about this café to be healed from old wounds and cynicism about this world.

From a simple cup of Rwandan black tea, the underlying principles of our new social enterprise float to the surface like leaves in a gentle tide. We will be hospitable, following *chado*, listening to the stories as we begin to heal. We will serve up justice tea that may free more women. That is how to dream a cup of tea. We take in the rich history, see the steam like the mist of Rwandan mountains, and as the warm liquid fills the body, we let our hearts turn to flesh. In that vulnerable moment, we can believe that together we can live in a more loving world.

But I am also grateful that while I dwell in this cup of tea from Rwanda and dream, no one can read my private thoughts like leaves in the bottom of a cup. I am sure that my private worries, doubts, and longings are written on my brow, but they remain mine. Tea can carry the dreams, and it can hold my thoughts that rise without permission like steam from the deep place of longing. It is good that tea can be a confessor throughout this journey. It can hold my thoughts and let them steep as I fantasize about how good my life would be in the hills of Rwanda alongside the pioneers working with women to bring justice and tea together. A friend and I would get up early and brew a pot of tea from a large tin pan over an open fire. The misty hills would sit with us like a warm blanket. We would go out and start a quiet revolution while building community and living simply, as the world loved us. Tea can take our fantasies without judgment, and it's not like taking a good long look in the mirror. In a cup of tea you can be any age and pull memories off the shelf and dream of a better you. It is freedom to dream a cup and then be refreshed enough to empty out the leaves and get back to work.

*Chapter Three*

# DRINKING TEA IN COMMUNITY

## Milk Thistle Recipe

Milk thistle, a plant belonging to the same family as daisies, is native to the Mediterranean regions and grows in Europe, North America, South America, and Australia. Milk thistle has been used for thousands of years in Europe to restore and detoxify the liver. After trauma, it settles the body to a needed balance. The seeds contain the antioxidant silymarin, which has health benefits. Thistle tea improves digestion and strengthens the immune system. The thistles are a symbol of hope for us at Thistle Farms and keep us on solid ground, ground that once felt cracked and parched. All parts of the milk thistle plant have been eaten as food, and its seeds have been used for a drink similar to coffee.

Milk thistle tea blends are available at gourmet and specialty stores, but a less expensive, healthier, and tastier option is to create your own. Combine 2 tablespoons milk thistle seeds with 2 tablespoons cardamom pod seeds and 2 tablespoons dandelion root. (All ingredients can be purchased online.) Smash this mixture with a back of a spoon or pestle. Avoid grinding it into dust. Add this blend to 3 tablespoons of your favorite basic loose-leaf China green tea. Steep 1 tablespoon per cup for 5 minutes. Enjoy.

Herbal teas are not teas in the strictest sense of the word but simply tisanes. They are hot beverages made from herbs, leaves, and roots of plants, but they do not contain the actual tea plant. They can have wonderful tea qualities to them—of offering a rich, hot flavor—and your senses react to herbal tinctures much the same as to tea. There are chamomile, thistle, lavender, and countless other herbal teas to choose from. They are organic and reek of the earth. They steep in humility like all wild medicines and are good for our minds, bodies, and souls. Growing and serving herbal teas are essential to what the café stands for. They offer healing from the earth and make us aware of how the way we eat helps us move toward wholeness.

GROWING THISTLE FARMS, INCLUDING the new café venture, has long required me to be on the road telling our story and securing funding, but as I checked into a small-town hotel in the Shenandoah Valley of West Virginia, an old and all-too-familiar fear rushed through me. It is a fear that I have kept close as I have grown organizations and churches. There are times when things are so lean that you can feel the skin of your teeth. Over the years I have heard all the things that fear was whispering into my head that day: *What if this new group of strangers don't have the slightest interest in helping? What if Thistle Farms loses money and we have to lay off employees who feel the security of a paycheck for the first time in their lives?*

I looked past the check-in clerk and into the reflection of fear I saw in the huge mirror behind his head, thanked him for the room keys, and left, determined to quiet my anxiety before speaking. Over the years I've discovered that whenever those negative thoughts swirl inside my head, I need to start walking. Something about walking moves a heart away from fear and toward freedom. Walking through town, I discovered a coffee and tea shop that greeted visitors with a sign that said, "You're welcome here!" Those three words were like a blanket of comfort to a wandering pilgrim in search of community. They also reminded me that sometimes we imagine that our visions are new insights, when we are merely stepping into old truths that are just new to us. I ordered a berry herbal tea blend and held the mug against my chest, feeling its warmth pour into my soul. The hot herbal drink quenched my thirst even though it was muggy outside. Though it might seem counterintuitive to drink a hot beverage on such a day, the truth is that while tea warms you in winter, it also cools you on warmer days. Sipping herbal tea can give you a cooling peace even on lonely and anxiety-laden afternoons. Tea can quiet voices of worry and fear long enough for a more rational frame of mind to take hold.

A volunteer at Thistle Farms recently shared how a community helped her quiet her fears and heal:

*I walked a path of solitude, abandonment, and sexual abuse from toddlerhood to early adulthood. Along the frightful darkness of my unchosen path came moments of hope, faith, and love. These splashes of "rays" provided the foundation of resilience and courage necessary to survive each day. Though the path I walk today is full of happiness and sunshine, the journey of healing is an ongoing reality that demands my honesty, fearlessness, and compassion.*

*The continued love and support of my beautiful daughters, loving husband, family, and friends humbles me each and every day. Upon receiving a Thistle Farms gift from my oldest daughter several years back, my passionate desire to become a Thistle Farmer has graciously become a reality. What a serendipitous moment to walk through Thistle Farms' doors after retiring from thirty-six years in the food industry, just in time to share my experience and be a part of opening the Thistle Stop Cafe.*

—Kathy Nelson

Tea was my companion on that muggy afternoon alone in the hills of West Virginia. It dawned on me as I drained the last bit of berry herbs that Thistle Farms was becoming a whole village. Like tea, people are a blend of complexity and simplicity. Alone, sometimes we are left with our own anxiety, and sometimes in that space our dreams can't be sustained. But gathered together as a community, people have immeasurable power and potential for doing good. Many of the volunteers share the same longing for community where their own private fears can be quieted and where they can be nurtured by others who welcome them into a circle of hope.

We need to be able to serve tea and say "welcome" as a whole community. Thistle Farms is already sewing, making paper, and making bath and body care products. It is now time to welcome strangers every week into our midst with a beautiful cup of tea as each wanders in from the internal and external hithers and yons of this world. We touch a global community whenever we touch or serve tea. We are touching the sweat and work of pickers and cultivators and shippers and retailers from places we have never seen. In the café we drink from a cup offered as treasure from a fellow pilgrim we've never met. This practice of drinking tea connects us around the world and back to our hearts as we make our way into the new space. Serving tea will be a way for us to help individuals birth new communities of hope around the world.

While our deepest fears cannot be extinguished just by the gift of community, it is the daily medicine that helps us walk through the fears we have to face alone. Julian of Norwich summed up the nature of that path beautifully seven hundred years ago when she wrote in *Revelations of Divine Love*: "If there is anywhere on earth a lover of God is always kept safe, I know nothing of it, for it was not shown to me. But in falling and rising again we are always kept in that same precious love."[9] Love, found in the gift of a community, will be with us after we succeed or if we fail, but we are not guaranteed a carefree and safe path just because we love. This way of tea is grounded in love, but it is not without cost.

When I returned from the beautiful valley where hills roll and strangers offered encouragement and financial help to start this new venture, I began to pour more and more tea. By mid-March we knew we needed a quarter of a million dollars to see a café come to life. My hope had been to raise a hundred thousand dollars. As projects find communities and communities have ideas, things get more complicated. We had doubled the size and scope of the project so that the café could meet the size of the need. It was a lot to take in, because I knew it meant we had to do all the demolishing, floor laying, deck building, and painting ourselves to keep construction costs down so we would have enough in our coffers to open with equipment and inventory.

I have learned much from years of working with committees and teams of people who feel strongly about things and don't shy away from expressing their convictions. Individual expression is a good thing as a sign of communal buy-in to the vision. When I first launched the Magdalene community, I struggled at night to figure out how we could ever move forward without hurting someone's feelings. It's a tricky road because there's nothing worse than design by committee. I have sat through committee meetings that feel as crazy as loose tea in a pot of hot water when it floats in wild, uneven patterns. But I also believe in the inspired nature of community. Community is a gift in which the sum is greater than its parts. The entity of community is what keeps us accountable and holds us up when we need support. Groups of people force us to think bigger and come to a new place of understanding.

Committees or teams can become a hindrance when you have to wait for everyone to agree on things like logos, menu selection, and colors. A team where everyone has to agree on every last detail can kill the life of a muse and weaken the most fervent of leaders. There have been times when we have waited for weeks for people to agree on colors for candles or scents for oils in our manufacturing facility. The best way we've found to work together is to allow everyone to express their opinion, including the person with actual design and architectural work experience. After all the ideas are offered, the one person designated as the designer is allowed to move forward.

Tea has been through the journey of individual inspiration and community decision making a million times. It has been blended, cured, baked, bricked, and dried, just to suit the particular fancy of the owner. Tea has been watered down, broken, and smuggled by groups that used it for its own purposes. How tea has come to be what it is has been due in some ways to the particular preference or vision of the person manipulating the leaves and/or the company refining them to withstand disease, weather conditions, and pestilence. If the goal of our café is to serve justice and freedom with tea, I am happy to surrender my personal opinion on design so we can walk peaceably to higher ground. We will each have areas we excel in and areas in which we may have a personal opinion that is just that—a personal opinion.

The end result of communities working on growing, producing, and trading tea for more than three thousand years is that tea takes on countless different personalities, depending on the personality of the person in charge. Each tea made in a certain region at a certain period by a certain cultivator becomes unique and carries a signature. Like a fine wine, it is formed by *terroir*, a region's soil and climate. When you sip a cup of tea, it might have been grown in India, China, Sri Lanka, Kenya, Ecuador, Japan, China, or any of the other twenty countries now producing tea. It could have traveled a greater part of the 25,000 miles in less than twenty-four hours on the modern tea routes that link the whole world. Each tea tastes and smells unique, and each has been handled by hundreds of individuals in a chain of markets to bring you a tea by a larger committee.

That is how I hope it will be with the café. Though connected in some ways to every other cafe, it will look and feel different. The store will have its own *terroir* because of the community who created it and the community who frequents it. In some ways, that *terroir* lies at the core of all successful social endeavors. They're connected to the universal, are steeped in local ground, and uphold our ideals of justice.

It seems like a dream that a simple, earthy, and welcoming community could help women who have almost always felt the scales of justice tip away from them. The communities that most of the women of Magdalene grew up in worked against them. For hundreds of years, the vast majority of tea that has been consumed in this world reeked of injustice because of the way it was grown, picked, processed, and traded. Two examples of how tea was linked to human trafficking include the treatment of Tamals in Ceylon in the late nineteenth century, and the forced labor of people in India after the East India Company ceased the slave trade.[10] Stories such as these make tea a hard drink to swallow sometimes. These two examples of injustice have been going on for centuries.[11] While people were sipping tea in England in the eighteenth and nineteenth centuries, slave labor and drug trafficking were helping manufacture and transport this civilized drink.[12] In the 1840s, Britain started the Opium Wars, and after a victory over China, new ports opened that allowed the smuggling of tea seeds and manufacturing processes to England. In order for England to grow tea in

India that could compete with tea from China, England stole secrets and hired spies like Robert Fortune to learn how to process tea leaves, and broke trust and treaties to use the tea market for their own gain.

The greedy trading community left tea laborers in poverty while they racked up profits of as much as 1,000 percent. The tragedy of trading tea for opium and illegal smuggling to avoid taxes links tea to trafficking and addiction. This link connects the work of Thistle Stop Café even more closely to the world of tea. It makes the serving of tea by survivors of trafficking and prostitution more significant.

The roots of human trafficking are fed by the world of drugs and housed in the human construct of poverty, just like tea. Thousands of young women are trafficked and prostituted annually. Now is the right time to call the community together and open the first café that reaches across the world to restore tea and the women serving it. This awareness combined with the serving of justice tea by women who know what injustice feels and tastes like will help us move into the national movement we long to be. The women and girls who have survived trafficking and prostitution need community to heal. Because they do not heal without economic independence, there is a great need for more social enterprises in communities where the ongoing well-being of the workforce is the primary mission and survivors are able to earn living wages.

This café, if done well, might help the national conversation regarding trafficking and prostitution. Rereading that line, I recognize that this language sounds so much bigger than the reality of opening a café, but tea demands a large contextual setting. Drinking tea allows us to be poetic and think big. The café can offer a sense of place. From these walls we can launch national podcasts, a Shared Trade Alliance, a growing workforce, flash tea parties, and awareness campaigns to help bring more communities to action. I feel strong as I dream of a cup of tea being served from that space. We need to feel small things strongly to keep big things moving forward.

The women who will serve this tea will have spent, on average, ten years on the street prostituting themselves to support addictions and have lengthy records of arrest or incarceration. We know before we even meet them that they will have experienced physical and sexual assault and will have been trafficked on the dead-end street where poverty runs into the wall of justice. Fired up by the history of injustice in tea and trafficking, we can't wait to open a beautiful sanctuary that serves up justice with every cup. The community that helped harm the women and trade tea unfairly can damn well help heal the women, too.

This conviction and passion are the launching pad for inspiration to move into a full-fledged fundraising effort and bring this dream to fruition. Much of the money donated so far is from women who love the idea of a café. They may be in recovery, they may come from a farm, their moms may have loved tea, but they see this as a place honoring every woman's story and hope. The café appeals to a sense of justice, with a bit of ambiance. In general, capital money is easier to raise than program money. It is easier for folks to think about starting something new as opposed to paying for the old. I love the stories that are coming in with the donations and find that there are more people out there than I ever imagined who want to taste justice tea poured in hope into a beautiful old teacup.

Every so often I catch a glimpse of the difference this café will make in the lives of the women. I recently took a walk through the woods with a graduate of the Magdalene program I hadn't seen in a while. I brought along two cups of tea steeped to a perfect golden brown. As we were walking and talking about the reality of this café, I realized we were sharing a communion with the birds and flowers. We had slowed our pace, had taken tiny sips of tea, and were almost whispering our conversation like a prayer. The space was like an altar for St. Francis or a tea set with perfect floral arrangements: vivid greens and the stunning blend of butter yellow and periwinkle that makes the back of your teeth clench with joy. She told me while we were walking that tea was coming into her life when she needed a new good habit. She said she had given up so much to be a part of this community, it was nice to welcome something she could take on with no guilt.

It's as if tea can't help itself. In its pure simplicity, it calls you to slow down, to pay attention, and to listen. As we were walking, we traveled back to her past, talked about her future longings, and dreamed of what the café might be like. After the walk, I thought about the gift of having time. Time is the gift we offer when we think we have tons of it. We can lavish time on friends and listen to their stories and walk and sip tea. It's when time feels scarce that we make a run on it like rationed gas and find ourselves with less and less of it to spare. Tea opens us the time to have the conversation that brings us to intimacy and community with our tea-drinking friends.

*The woman who birthed me was twelve when I was born in 1982. She had six more children and all of us were placed in foster care. I only know one of my siblings. I was in and out of seven different foster homes. I don't remember having friends or toys, just being molested in each home. I didn't know that was wrong because no one told me. I never spoke a word. I held it all in. I went up for adoption to a better home with nice people. She wanted me to call her Mom. In the other homes there was no such word as "Mom"!*

*The lady didn't know what she was getting herself into when she adopted my sister and me. I came with a lot of baggage and was unable to receive love from others. It was like a foreign language. She tried, and I had good food to eat, a nice home, and nice things. Then her brothers came down from Detroit and babysat us while Mom was working overtime. I was molested again, and I still didn't know I should tell someone. My behavior became very bad. I would get in fights at school. I'd see someone getting picked on and I felt the need to step in, I think because I wished for the longest time someone would step in and help me. One day in class a teacher talked about adults touching you. She*

53

*said it was wrong and that you should tell someone. I had never heard that. I spoke to her because I felt like holding that information inside was killing me softly. When my mom found out, she blamed it on me, and it felt like she didn't want to deal with it. I ran away at the age of fifteen, mad at the world. One thing I knew was I knew how to please men. I ran with that.*

*Before my eighteenth birthday, I was getting high every day and neglecting the two children I had birthed. My kids were placed with friends of mine. I lost my home and went to the streets. That's when I learned quickly how to survive and not get run over. I had to do what I had to do to get quick money for my drug habit. This went on for years and years. I got arrested and looked at jail as a place of rest. I got a felony for selling drugs and served nine months. I went back out on paper, didn't do the right thing, and ended up back in jail for eleven months. That is when I sat down and asked God to come into my life and help me stay clean. I got into all the programs and classes to help me become a better person on the inside.*

*While I was in jail, I wrote the Magdalene program asking for help. The whole time I was working on the issues of my past. Today, I believe the story is not over in my life. God allowed me to go through things only to carry me from them and be a help to others. He was working in my life and I'm glad my past didn't dictate the ending of my story.*

*—Anika*

*Chapter Four*

# TEA RITUALS

## Monkey Tea

Yunnan golden monkey tea has a sweet bouquet and is the color of amber. It draws you in because the name is so appealing. No one is sure if that wonderful name came from the monkeys that may have picked leaves that grew high on uncultivated plants or because the leaves look hairy, much like the monkeys that live in the Yunnan region of China, where the first known tea trees grew. When you drink this tea, you can imagine tasting a connection back to some of the first known cultivated plants. It is the perfect tea to sip as you contemplate ritual and the old gift found anew in tea.

The best way to prepare this tea is to first purchase the leaves from producers that you have researched and believe are concerned about the workers as well as the quality of the plant. The best water temperature for this black tea is about 200 degrees, and you should let about 1 teaspoon steep for 3 minutes in a small pot of water. The color of this tea is so beautiful that serving it in a white china teacup enhances the experience.

SOMETIMES WHEN I DRINK tea, it's as if I'm smelling sacred incense or feeling a well-worn quilt. As I take the first sip of a steamy cup, it's like calling on the old saints to come and share their wisdom. Whenever I read about tea, I'm reminded that I'm studying a sacred history that carries one of the oldest cultivated plants known as both a symbol and a practical tool. When we smell tea, we are sharing in the experience of monks in Japan more than thirteen hundred years ago. The story of tea is so revered that there are myths that the Buddha himself made the first cup and shared it with his followers. Because tea is laden with ritual, tea and religion have always been intertwined. This is significant because tea, in addition to being a drink, is also a symbol of the universal thirst for spirit and truth. As the second most popular liquid consumed worldwide next to water, tea has a rare podium from which to preach about global connectedness and peace in this world.

The world of tea was held in such high esteem that it was a protected secret for more than two thousand years. Until the nineteenth century, it was still believed in England that green and black tea leaves came from two different plants, instead of being the result of different manufacturing processes. It was a mysterious elixir that people longed for, and learning how to drink it properly and with ritual was compelling.

The nature and effects of tea lend themselves to use in

religious practices and rituals. Cultivation, preparation, and serving tea provide physical and spiritual benefits. This quieting and clarifying drink offers a natural way to focus your mind, body, and spirit. All of the accouterments, such as tending tea gardens or setting the tea service, offer us a path for learning discipline, cultivation, patience, and faithfulness.

Over the centuries, tea became a currency in the East as it moved into Japan, Mongolia, and Tibet. One could trade tea for horses and pay tribute to dynasty leaders in bricks of tea. Monks and gardeners dedicated large parts of their daily practice to the tending the tea plants and to refining the planting, growing, and processing of the leaves. In the eighth century AD, China began the tradition of formal tea gatherings and developed the role of the tea master. Through years of study and practice, this master embodied the way of tea culture and etiquette and can guide students and pilgrims. This is the time when Lu Yu, considered one of the fathers of tea, wrote the masterpiece *The Classic of Tea*, also known as *Ch'a Ching*. This magnum opus remains one of the most quoted texts in the world of tea literature. In it Lu Yu explores the tools and utensils of tea, including the precise details of boiling.

At times the story of Lu Yu's life reads more like fiction than fact. Tea lore suggests he was adopted by a Buddhist monk and later ran off to the circus as a clown. He found favor with a local governor who offered him access to his library and a teacher. Lu Yu eventually learned the arts of calligraphy, poetry, and tea. He dedicated his life to the perfection of growing, manufacturing, and serving tea. *The*

*Classic of Tea* establishes an unbroken line from the first tea leaves to the cup we sip from in the present. It solidifies the connection between drinking tea and the religious experience as it ties the leaves to the fathers of tea, the growers and pickers of the leaves, and the experience of drinking tea in a deep, awe-filled ritual.

The relationship between tea and religion remains strong throughout the world today. Tea ceremonies range from Eastern practices, to a maté experience in South America where yerba maté is served from seasoned gourds, to a high tea with rare stoneware in a more Western ritual, to a South African bush tea around a ceremonial fire. Websites, newsletters, hundreds of Twitter accounts, and books by tea communities around the world want to help usher in a revival of tea reverence around the world. Some people go so far as to drink only teas that come directly from living plants without drying the leaves because they offer true healing to our bodies. A global community of tea drinkers is discovering that the way of tea is opening a path to justice. There is a growing economic market for tea grounded in the deep respect for the ritual of appreciating and sharing the beverage.

To understand the connection between tea and religious rituals, I needed to attend more formal tea ceremonies. I know from my twenty-five years as a priest the value of setting a table and offering a ritualized meal. A kinship exists between setting an altar with fine linen and setting a tea table with a cloth. Chalices and patens, teacups and saucers seem copacetic. I could learn about the story of tea like I learned the art of presiding at religious services and rites. I could learn from experts, I could experiment and imitate my mother's habits, improvising when I needed to.

One of the first rituals I attended was a Japanese tea ceremony in the botanical gardens of Seattle. This event is highly regarded among tea aficionados. As I walked the path toward the ceremony, it felt clear that the way of tea is meant to lead us with intention toward peace. The circuitous route leading to the small building where the ceremony was held was lined with carefully placed rocks, small ponds, and ornamental statues. The location of every plant was calculated. Every detail had a meaning. I walked with my senses wide awake and wide aware as I took in the details of the light and the space. I knew I needed more language, more history, more context to understand all the layers of meaning, but even with my limited knowledge, I could sense the beauty and meaning in the deepest parts of my being.

Among the first acts in a tea ceremony is the presentation of *matcha*, the powered green tea whipped into a bitter liquid. We admired the artistry and beauty as each bowl and utensil was set out for viewing. Time was spent cleansing pots, pans, and whisks, followed by a ritualized cleansing of the person serving the tea. Each participant practiced gratitude and awareness throughout the ceremony as they knelt and watched.

As the lead tea server knelt before the elements of tea and purified herself, I was reminded of a fellow priest preparing the Eucharist at an altar. The similarities between these purification rituals are striking. Both are done in public view with the intention of cleansing the servers before they touch the sacred elements. By pouring water over their hands and being careful not to touch anything unclean before they serve, they are showing honor through humility. Both acts remind those involved that presiders at the rites are to serve with right intentions.

After the servers were cleansed, they bowed as they placed the tea in front of us, the receivers of tea. We returned the gesture and bowed from our kneeling position in gratitude. Images of churchgoers bounced in my mind, as they genuflect before the altar and kneel in pews after receiving communion. Both the tea ceremony and the Eucharistic meal are social events that stress aesthetics and require appreciation of long-standing traditions. Bowing as I took my first sip reminded me of the beauty I take for granted in my own religious tradition. Both rituals ask participants to believe that in the practice we become what we hope to be—more at peace and closer to God.

The act of preparing and pouring tea can take long enough to make the tea service the entire focus of the gathering. It slows time and stretches out moments to be fully experienced. Watching the presiders at this meal made me want to be more intentional about how I serve communion. Slowing the serving of the bread and wine would be a gift. Partakers might find moments stretched and feel the stone places in their hearts melting.

But ritual cuts both ways in hearts. Just as the grace and wonder of ritual were allowing me to be more mindful, I glanced at the women servers walking in small steps with cinched robes and remembered that with every ritual meal, there are traps. I am torn by the truth that even this beautiful and almost silent ritual carries the note of oppression on the tails of the obis the women don. Whenever we participate in religious ceremonies, we know that a history including oppressive behaviors toward women is not that far behind. The servers of tea wear the traditional kimonos of the geisha, who served tea as part of their rituals. In addition to being entertainers and servers, the geisha have a history of exploitation and abuse. My mental struggle lingered as I knelt for another forty-five minutes. The thoughts of beauty and oppression hung in the silent air as I admired the bowls, watched the generosity, and tasted the sweet homemade rice cake.

At the end of the ceremony, the guests were invited to slurp the last sip of tea that became froth at the bottom of the cup. I want to slurp the last drop as part of the tradition of the *chado*. I want to participate in this beautiful dance of tea without judgment. But it is hard not to let the historical oppression of women seep into the steeping frothy tea. Beauty and ritual are forever tied into the images of women that keep them from the fullest expressions of being human. At least that is how it feels sometimes. Keep women veiled and cinched and silent, and then they will be honored. In witnessing the scene before me, I know that the women who will work in the café will have borne the brutality of the world. I am too keenly aware that faith and ritual can truly be the ties that bind us to violence and complacency.

But I am just a student of tea. I was only in a position on my knees to reflect and could not let my projections blind me to the beauty unfolding before me. There will be a time to raise our teacups and shout that we are ready for a new revolution. We will proclaim we are ready to change this world that still buys and sells women, we are ready to change the way we consume so that small farmers receive living wages and the land thrives, and we are ready to pour our resources and time into healing structures like the café and break down the prison walls. But that time hasn't come. So I slurp my last sip of tea with the host and keep walking the way of tea.

After the tea ceremony finished, I felt the pull of tradition, one that begs you to live more acutely and intentionally. While tea never talks back, I can almost hear the distant past calling me to learn more. In recent years, I've discovered that the rituals around the tea, whether in a traditional ceremony or in a more personal practice, are good habits to develop for all spiritual travels.

Another ritual that I've tried to embrace through the tea ceremony is the practice of waiting. Nothing about the ceremony is ever rushed. Everything moves in a holy hush of slow motion. Every action is deliberate, every cell of energy well spent. One of the ways to embrace the slowing in tea culture comes from a tea called herbal florals. This Chinese luxury tea is made from tying, with a small white string, teas, herbs, and dried flower into a large dry blossom sculpted into a ball. As you drop the tightly wound ball of tea into hot water you can sit and watch the tea slowly come to life in the water. Dried petals unfurl leaf by leaf like a resurrection fern on a summer day. The watery play of the dancing flower turns the water to sepia as a magical blossom appears from the middle of the flower that once hid its treasure. It grows and dances with stray petals and saturated leaves. When it has taken its final bow, I'm invited to drink it in. Somehow I never feel like I'm waiting during the steeping, even though time has passed. Instead it is a joyful dance of unfolding mystery. Whenever I use an herbal floral, some of that joy sinks into my heart. The ritual of waiting produces the fruits of unexpected peace that I am invited to drink in along with the joy of expectation.

Learning to pay attention to the small details is another free and unending gift the rituals of tea ceremony can teach. Not too long ago I sat at a gate at the airport and put a floral tea ball into steamy hot water and sat down. I opened my e-mail as I watched the tea turn an ordinary cup of water into a black, deep brew. One of the employees at Thistle Farms had written an e-mail about our sage field that we had recently planted and tended and why they had decided not to harvest the sage leaves the day before, as scheduled. She wrote that the plants looked withered and she wanted me to see the field before they did anything. This was sad news. Not only had Thistle Farms made a significant investment in time and plants, but the sage had been expected to double in size. Instead, it was dying, and my hopes of harvesting the leaves and turning them into essential oils were shriveling. I could picture the sage rolling into small dried, lifeless balls that looked like the tea I was drinking.

In the face of disappointment, the rituals I learned from the way of tea offered peace and clarity. They gave me the path to simply take in the news and sip my tea. Breathe. And lean in to the grieving. My heart sank as I imagined the lost, blackened crop. I hate it when things you count on start to fall apart. After another sip, another breath, I kept reading the e-mail. "Remember, all is not lost. We did our best, and that is all anyone could have expected," she wrote. "We had some memorable experiences and on the drive we saw wild turkeys and wildflowers cutting through the morning mist. We were once again reminded that it is not the destination but the journey—and this is as true in sage fields as it is with our lives."

With my next sip I drank to the women who reminded me of these eternal truths. Though my mind and emotions were tempted to just see lost revenue that would slow the building of our business and the launch of the café, the journey of healing with a community was far more important, and making the journey well requires waiting. The women of Thistle Farms know the significance of waiting well: All the years of waiting to be released from prison, all the time spent walking the streets waiting to be picked up, all the waiting for change becomes the grounding for the hard work of healing. The sage is struggling and I want to get back to it as soon as I can, but it can wait and I can choose to be at peace right here, right now.

The ritual of tea, whether in a formal ceremony or sipped with intention to wait in peace on the way to another event, enhances the experience of one of the world's oldest brews. Bad habits and rituals can hold us back like oppressive old histories that keep us from enjoying the cup right before us.

Rituals get us back on track and remind us there is always something new to learn, discover, and incorporate into our very own tea rituals. Within an expanding ritual around tea, you'll find new depths of your spirit in your breath over the steam, in the reflective vision of your gaze, and in the ability to hold on to a single moment as if it were eternity itself. Ritual makes fresh the ancient way and can lead us to a new place that is like an old home we have been searching for. Rituals remind us that our path doesn't have to be complicated to be rich. It doesn't require tons of maps and manipulations to be beautiful. A simple old path walking toward justice is our calling. We are urged on by the hope that, if we keep walking, we will keep following a tea path garden by a small creek and maybe someday reach a river where justice rolls. We can keep following the good rituals that can free us and bring justice and freedom to all parts of the world.

## A Basic Tea Ritual

A basic ritual for serving tea I learned from friends and my family is always have a heated kettle that lives near the burner as the prologue to a visit.

Then you begin the ritual by choosing a tea based on the ambiance you want to create. Make sure that its leaves and roots are linked to the kind of justice you want to be a part of. Many people believe a basic black tea is the only tea to serve. I am by nature and constitution drawn to the lighter green teas. Take a little scalding water from the kettle, pour it into the pot, and swirl it around to clean and heat the teapot. Then dump that water out, fill the teapot with the hot water to the top, and add tea. Let the tea steep for 3 to 5 minutes and pour it into the cups. This ritual will prepare and steep the group as well as the tea.

The kettle itself is a signal that there's time to talk. People can slow down and wait as the minutes unfold slowly enough that you can hold them. When the tea is steeped you can start the real conversation; otherwise you have rushed things. The best part of the simple tea ritual to me is the first sip and the anticipation of the temperature and taste. You watch the people you are sharing tea with for judgment or affirmation. If the tea is bitter, it might be a sign. If it's mellow, that might be one, too. Drink the broth and make conversation with thoughts that can be as mellow or as bitter as the tea before you. Drink it knowing that the water that courses through your body has been transformed. It is still water, but now it holds the fragrance of earth and people. It holds healing, and it holds history. Learning to serve tea and participate in the ritual of tea drinking is a fundamental part of the way of tea. It opens the gifts of tea's ability to connect and restore us.

*Chapter Five*

# TEA'S MYSTERIOUS CALLING

## A White Tea Blend

One of the purest and oldest teas is white tea. White tea is dried without any fermentation and is the least processed of any tea. It is picked early in the year while the tiny white hairs are still visible on the leaves and the bud is still closed. Only the top leaf and a bud are picked from the plant. The leaves dry in the sun briefly.

White tea is perfect blended with organic fruits and flowers. One of my favorite combinations is blueberries and dried cornflowers mixed into the tea. Buy white teas already blended or mix dried flowers and fruits into the blend yourself.

# THE WAY OF TEA AND JUSTICE

Heat water to 175 degrees.

Steep the white tea in the pot for just 1 to 2 minutes.

Serve with a bit of honey if desired to keep the beautiful and light flavor.

A GROUP FROM THISTLE FARMS returned from a week in England where we participated in a global conference. For two of the women, it was their first journey overseas. They didn't even think about jet lag when their feet touched the ground. They headed off on a double-decker bus to see the palace, where they waved the Union Jack. The conference itself was a beautiful gathering of twenty thousand folks committed to working for justice and peace. Healing happens one person at a time in the small local work of the thousand groups gathered that together seemed like a grassroots movement big enough to change the balance of love in the world. Those small communities all gathered together embodied the idea that hope itself can make a difference. In addition to the conference, it was a great gift that Marcus, my beloved husband, was able to play music and take a couple of days off to share tea with me in some of the oldest teahouses and pubs in the Western world. England is a mecca of tea. Traveling there to drink tea is like heading to Rome to see an old church or going to Peru to see ruins.

England is steeped in tea culture. Tea was introduced to England by the Dutch in the seventeenth century. Soon the love of tea spread to Ireland and Scotland, where today more tea per capita is consumed than anywhere else in the world. Teahouses began in the eighteenth century and ensured tea's place as part of the social and political culture of England.

At the end of the conference, my husband and I took a train and stayed in Oxford. The first day, we took afternoon tea in an old, famous pub called the Eagle and Child. This pub opened in the seventeenth century and is famous for being the home pub of a group of writers and scholars known as the Inklings. The two most famous members of the group are J.R.R. Tolkien and C. S. Lewis, who became friends while they were both professors. I sat at the table next to where the sign said they sat. I let my Earl Grey tea steep in the history of the place where they talked about theology and fantasy and interwove them into a sacred space called story. The pub itself was dark and old, and it was easy to move out of time as I sipped the rich black tea. The oak floor, benches, walls, and tables were blackened by time and cigar ash and aged in such a graceful way that they looked like holy relics.

Drinking tea and daydreaming as I leaned against the dark paneled walls, I half expected to see Tolkien and Lewis saunter in and begin a conversation that carried them through long, rainy afternoons. Friends coming by to sate their thirst for banter, I imagined, might interrupt their conversation from time to time. In one of the scars on the flooring beside their table, I imagined Tolkien leaning his chair back whenever Lewis offered a thought that felt too provincial to Tolkien. The leaning back on two legs time after time finally dented the floor. Maybe the scar on the floor on the other side of the table came from Lewis pushing the table away to stretch as Tolkien began reading. Those scars felt like outward and visible signs that Tolkien and Lewis were still present in this place through their ideas and works that have outlived them.

They probably entered the pub after walking along the sidewalk past the cemetery of St. Giles' Church just down the street. This church is almost a thousand years old and has its own graveyard. The tombstones in the yard are so old that lichens are the only markings left on many. Maybe the walk by those old stones was the procession that fueled Tolkien and Lewis to write powerfully and poetically enough to find immortality and be spared the truth that even head-stones return to dust eventually. I imagine that when they left the pub, their conversations played over in their minds as they went back to the lonely task of writing and editing. I love that in this pot of tea, a story has poured out and that its aroma mixed with the scent of blackened oak carries us out of time and into imagination.

Sitting under the influence of great writers, I sipped my tea as slowly as I could, almost tasting my fate. My fate, like that of all of us, is to lie beneath a stone whose lettering will eventually wear off so that we rest in peace. When we let it sink into the back of our heart it leaves us shaking in the valley of the shadow of death. The thought reminds us that we want to live our best with the time we have been given and to savor every single cup of tea we are allowed to taste. In my mind, I can hear Lewis and Tolkien talking about death and life for hours. Somehow the echoes of their conversations bring a sweet taste to what might otherwise be a bitter broth.

If people like Tolkien and Lewis had been daunted by their own mortality and had not believed in the hope of eternal love, this pub and these old black floors may have been forsaken a long time ago. If they had not faced their own mortality with courage, our lives would be poorer. If they had not dared to contemplate the hardest questions of theology and just thrown a pint back to ward off thought, they never would have dreamed of *Lord of the Rings* or *The Lion, the Witch and the Wardrobe.*

Their lives call us to imagine, over a pot of tea, not just them but the whole universe and God. When our imagination conjures up hope and heroic acts of love in the face of death, we are moved to action. Tolkien and Lewis knew death, yet they lived with amazing imaginations and allowed their ideas to grow in words on paper. History, time, and death call us to live deep in our imaginations and allow inspired action to move us undaunted. We are passing through and will share in the journey of becoming ashes. But before that journey, we are alive, and in our finitude we can imagine the infinite and unknown. We can imagine history and the future and be stirred by ghosts. We can hold an abiding hope through it all and be moved to do some of our greatest work. Hope seeps through scarred oak and dark tea.

Neither Lewis nor Tolkien had any idea that the path to Oxford was leading them to a deep friendship that would change their course forever. We rarely know that our friendships, made by circumstance and chance, offer us the opportunity to dream of new worlds where fanciful ideas of justice can thrive. The story of Lewis and Tolkien sharing tea and dreaming of new worlds emboldens all of us to dream big. Three minutes from the small pub is the thousand-year-old church dedicated to Mary Magdalen, the saint who symbolizes the healing power of love. She is depicted in beautiful and timeless stained glass overlooking the pub. For a millennium this shrine dedicated to the first preacher of the Gospels and the one for whom Jesus lingered at the tomb has been casting radiant light and reminding pilgrims that love can transform the world. Her image can carry weary mortal souls through the valley and lay them on the path of hope. She cries out to Lewis and Tolkien, you and I, that although injustices in this world seem immovable, with love all things can change and all hearts are flesh. She offers me a space to feel that even though the injustices associated with trafficking and tea are entrenched and continue to this day, we can hope and work toward a freer world. We don't have to be intimidated by what looks like unchangeable forces.

By the time I returned home, that inspiration had solidified into a plan called Shared Trade that would launch with the café. This new venture of Thistle Farms would be dedicated to fairer trade in the worlds of tea and social enterprises that employ women. The Shared Trade alliance would simply be a coalition of organizations focused on women and dedicated to bringing women permanently out of poverty through sustainable employment. Participating groups are enterprises trying to close the gap between producers and consumers in the value chain. Small and large social enterprises around the globe could come together in the alliance to share best practices and marketing strategies for economic leverage. We would act globally so women feel freedom locally. In other words, organizations working with women tea farmers in Uganda, or a sewing coopera- tive in Kenya, or an oil producer in Rwanda, or a café in Nashville would promise to work together to further all our endeavors while prioritizing work on increasing the wages of the working women.

Our notion of fair trade in tea is different from fair trade in other commodities like coffee or bananas. Fair trade in the world of tea is an underdeveloped path that has yielded to the historical precedent of servant labor established hun- dreds of years before. Fair trade is the official name of a federation that is building equitable and sustainable trad- ing partnerships and creating opportunities to alleviate pov- erty around the globe. Shared trade would be taking that notion a bit deeper as specific social enterprises dedicated to the workforce as the primary mission would go beyond the requirements of existing fair trade. Social enterprises in which women are both the workforce and the beneficiaries in the United States have, on average, three to five employees. That means that executive directors are also the marketers, trainers, and administrators. It also means that most of the organizations are underproducing, so it's hard for the strug- gling social enterprises to pay the women living wages or hours. By collectively and specifically supporting one another, we can help all our organizations. Through this new Shared

Trade initiative at Thistle Farms we would enable more small social enterprises that enable women to increase their economic leverage, train regional sales teams to promote one another's products, and develop branding power. When people see products stamped with Shared Trade, they will know that the work's mission is to help foster healing for women survivors. These goals will allow organizations in the alliance to have a marketing strategy to actually grow their companies and to increase their potential customers and donor database. One of the reasons why tea is picked by hand instead of with mechanical pickers is because traditionally the pickers are women with no political or social status.

Even in fair trade operations like in Sri Lanka, some workers live on land owned by companies that also own the school and health care, so they wield great power over the workers. Other workers in places like Kenya still live in poverty on dirt floors without access to clean water. I have seen tea pickers in rural communities in northern Kenya who still don't have enough money to buy school uniforms. Families must seek out not-for-profits to get the clothing their children need to attend grade school. Some argue that tea pickers are doing better than their poorer neighbors and that picking tea is an economic step up. But large tea corporations in Kenya and Sri Lanka have been documented as hiring pickers only on a temporary basis, so they never receive the benefits claimed by full-time company employees. There are stories of inadequate equipment and unsafe working conditions. Pesticides used by large tea companies compromise the health of the workers and the plants.

Formulating a shared trade idea, hiring a manager for the café, and finding new funding sources is bringing new life to the original idea. The idea of an alliance has given me hope that cup by cup we will get this venture going and move forward on this path.

In the midst of grand ideas there was still the issue that we needed to lay a new floor in the café area. The old floor had been ruined in the Nashville flood of 2010 and was unusable. We had to find a donor since our construction budget continued to increase just for all the electrical, plumbing, and new construction that needed to happen. The floor we found comes from an old tobacco warehouse owned by Al Gore's parents. It has been a huge job to lay it, sand it, and seal it, but that has worked itself out. The floor has now become part of the long and mysterious path by which this café came together, as these very beams began their journey 150 years ago when some tall red pines in California were hewn and brought to the hills of Tennessee. They will lie on this floor for decades to come, I hope, until they become as old and stained as the floors in the old Oxford pub. Maybe on these very floors, over a cup of a deep earth-colored tea, two people will begin a friendship that carries them to places they never would have dreamed of. Maybe one will write about a new world that the other happened to mention when describing a dream he or she had the night before. Maybe years later searching pilgrims will come and sit in the café where they heard these two friends were known to visit. Those young pilgrims will take note of the floor, of the old teacups, and carry the dream of hope out the door to another generation of people.

As we travel a path, there are moments, as in the pub in Oxford or standing by a whistling kettle, when we wake up to ourselves. Before that moment, we didn't know we were asleep. Afterward, we are startled to find out how long we were out. It's just like when you're driving down the road and can't remember how you got there. How do any of us get to where we are right now in the first place? How do any of us get to exactly right here? The path from there to here is not like Robert Frost's sweet image in his poem "The Road Not Taken" about choosing the simple single path others haven't worn out. When we wander around, it feels like the forks in the road are as complex as branches on an old oak tree.

The paths in our lives might begin with a single fork in the trunk of a tree at its base, but soon that fork has forks within forks until there are a thousand branches growing in different directions. The first paths aren't even paths we choose; they are chosen for us. Some are hidden or at least unknown to us. Paths can twist and turn until we end up on a road we can't find on a map or remember wanting to travel on. There we are, out on a limb, hanging on, and we can't remember how we got there.

In the twists and turns of the mysterious path, we awaken to that very moment and see clearly where we are on the road. In those moments, it's possible for the wild and shady roads to be the platform onto a new path of healing and hope. Self-reflection, community, ritual, and grace fuel such moments. I have seen women in the circle of Thistle Farms identify those moments on the path as a long process they recognize only when they see it in the rearview mirror. The knowledge that all paths can lead to wholeness and healing is of great comfort to me. It means no one lives outside the bounds of hope and all of us live within the borders of love. We can all find our way. In this context, healing becomes a sacramental walk toward wholeness. The hardest part is believing that we are heading somewhere holy as we are walking. Tea is such a great companion for pilgrims on the way and has been central to so many people on the journey. Its healing properties, warmth, aromatic gifts, and still-filled nature can be a great tool to help us awaken to ourselves and see where we are. Tea is the place where we can stop and become aware that all the forks in the road, all the blessings and brokenness, have led us to where we are and that where we are is a fine place to begin.

## The Cupping Room

Large tea companies have a place called the cupping room where tea makers sample the teas to be used. Tea sampling is very similar to wine tasting. The first step after placing the tea leaves in several cups around a table is to bring a spoonful of wet leaves up toward your nose. This is called nosing the leaf, and it is just taking a moment to inhale and allow the aroma of tea to entice your palate. Next tea is poured into small cups where the master taster notes the flavors and nuances of the tea. More than three hundred varieties of leaves can be blended with countless herbs and flowers. Tea masters have libraries in their heads that specify how each tea should taste. This knowledge takes expertise and years of practice and apprenticeship. The perfection of this art is a spiritual path of patience and awareness.

One of the Thistle Farms women, Dorris, describes living for twenty-six years and never leaving a ten-block radius. She thought she would end up somewhere different, but she kept ending up in the same spot. It began, she said, when, as a child, she witnessed the violent death of a parent. The trauma made the forks in the road impossible to discern. Fear and shame kept her pretty lost. But three years ago, she chose a different road and ended up at Magdalene, where she says that her road became a path of healing the past so she could move forward.

Dorris was on the same old path where she wore out her shoes and her body. The problem in waking up to yourself and finding a new path is that all new roads look frightening. Somehow, by God's grace, all of the roads both Dorris and I have traveled led us to the shore of the Gulf Coast. In all of the injustices she has seen and all of the searching she has done, her road less traveled never took her to the beach. It feels close to a miracle that our combined side roads crossed in that moment so I got to hold her hand as her feet touched the sugar sand for the first time. Her very first words were "Good job, God" as she tried to take in the whole gulf through eyes filled with tears. When she felt the pull of the waves on her feet she stretched out her arms and in a lilting voice asked, "Has it been doing this my whole life?" I thought, "My Lord, yes. As long as the moon has been orbiting the earth the tide has been coming. It just takes making our way to the shore to feel how powerful it is." While she was walking in circles for years, she had no idea that the tide, like love, has been pulling her toward freedom. I laughed as she bent down and picked up a seashell and said she couldn't believe that God put a hole in the shell just so she could string it on a necklace. It felt like a beautiful and simple thought that all roads lead to the shore eventually. Just then a blue heron flew and I felt the need to genuflect as its path to this shore was worth pondering as well.

It would be amazing to trace our journeys not just from our childhood or our own ancestry but to see where the path began, before the first fork in the road. If we could trace the path that far, then we could see the connection in the thousands of paths that are really all forks from a single path. Looking over that journey, we might get a better perspective on just how unbelievably random it is that we are here, in this fleeting moment, doing this exact thing.

As Dorris and I walked the beach, studying a piece of driftwood, I realized that the wood lying there is simply a limb from the many forks in the tree. Even the branch is fleeting. I was flooded with the thoughts of fleeting time like the waves coming into the shore. I wondered if the people walking along the sand sensed our connectedness and the randomness that had led us all to be on the beach at that exact moment in time.

It's no wonder there are so many ways to get off track and choose one fork that takes you flying toward a vulnerable north-exposed branch. But I was there on that beach, and I did not feel lost. Instead, being there was an answer to a long prayer. I felt grounded and knew that all the brokenness of my childhood, including the death of my father and the abuse by a church elder, were not outside the realm of grace. They were part of the first roots of the tree and my own first memory that serves as the trunk. Those memories and a million more allowed me to climb out onto this tender limb and see how love moves us. The thousand choices I have made led me to that moment on that stretch of beach and time that reminded me I was right where I was supposed to be; walking hand in hand with a woman feeling the eternal tide pull her toward love.

Few metaphors better capture this feeling than tea. As Dorris and I shared a cup of tea later and laughed about our experience, we are retracing forks in the road that lead back through a direct line a couple thousand years into the woods above the Mekong River in southwestern China. The path was as hard and dangerous as the path the woman beside me has walked. Many twists and turns of that path have inflicted pain. It was a path of exploitation and drugs, a path laden with misery and hardship. It was a path that led to new discovery, new enterprises, and new life. The path of going toward tea in the East is called the *roji*, or garden path. This path is critical to the experience of tea. It is peaceful and leads us to tea with intention.

The path of tea lies in juxtaposition to the wild and unintentional path the women at Thistle Farms have walked. There was nothing fair in the trade when they swapped their childhoods for the streets and sold their bodies for the numbing drugs that would help them forget the path they were on. Those traumas become the yellow brick road that leads to prison and wandering in circles. Sometimes our path is foisted upon us, and then the journey becomes how to make choices to heal from the path we were given. When someone argues that prostitution is a choice and I think about friends like Dorris, I always ask, "What were the other choices?"

*A graduate of the program talks with grace about the path she was given. She described it as "really, really, really rough." Her dad died from cancer and her mom was schizophrenic. She said people just came into their house and slept with her mom and abused her. She left for the streets to make her own way, she says, but truly her path was laid out before her.*

*When I was fourteen years old, I started using drugs and alcohol to cope with the things I was dealing* with in life. I lived in a very dysfunctional environment, and my mom was mentally ill. This caused me great pain because she was unable to care for my siblings and me. With all of the distress, I started medicating my agony and anger away with drugs and alcohol.

In addition, I started walking the streets all hours of the night and prostituting my body for money. I would jump in and out of cars with men I did not know. When I was finished I would have them drop me off at the next corner. As time went by, I became comfortable with the lifestyle that I was living, which lasted for fifteen years.

One day a guy that I had sex with for money introduced me to one of his friends. I was supposed to have sexual intercourse with him, but instead that person told me about the Magdalene program and Thistle Farms. After hearing about this, I made the phone call and immediately got into the program. That is when my life began to change. I received the help I needed and got a sponsor. I went to twelve-step meetings and the greatest thing happened to me: I found God, who became my best friend. He healed my mind, body, and spirit. He put back together what was broken into pieces, and now I know how to love others. Now I live the way God wants me to live.

Furthermore, I am blessed to say that I will be a proud employee of the Thistle Stop Café. When I walk into the café, I know that God's love endures forever right inside of every teacup that is held in someone's

*hand. There is a great story in everyone—a story that*
*can heal all self-destructive behavior and a story that*
*can save someone's life.*

—Anonymous

It's hard to face the times when it's not fight or flight, it's just us wrestling with our own shadows and making peace. On our spiritual path, this is the place we are eventually led to sit with ourselves and drink from the cup we have been offered. Love is in this cup, as it is in all the cups we have been given. It's time to taste it and figure out the next graceful step. No matter how any of us got where we are, our spiritual paths remind us we are in a good spot to learn about love. That is a universal truth that grounded us on the path to opening the new café.

We still need about 25 percent more capital, and our plans still need work. I pray new tea can be laid like bread crumbs along the way and not only lead women forward but help us find our way home. We talk at Thistle Farms quite often about how it is not a problem to be lost; it is only a problem if you think you can't find your way home. Tea can be a tool that helps us navigate the path, the *roji*, all the way back to our hearts. We can find ourselves on that path and make our way to sanctuary and safety. It is a spiritual axiom that old paths can lead us to new places. The old truth that Jesus preached about loving our neighbors led the disciples to walk a new way. It still calls us to walk the path that leads to a more just world.

## Chapter Six

# AROMATIC SWEET CUPS

## French Press Iced Peach Tea

Iced peach tea blend is the perfect tea for southern summers. The 1839 cookbook *The Kentucky Housewife*, by Mrs. Lettice Bryan, offered typical tea punch recipes found in cookbooks from the period such as making *tea punch* from a pint and a half of very strong tea the way you usually make it. Then strain the tea and pour it, still boiling onto 2½ cups of white sugar. Add half a pint of rich cream.

Another wonderful old recipe for southern sweet tea is from an 1879 community cookbook called *Housekeeping in Old Virginia*,[13] by Marion Cabell Tyree:

*Ice Tea—After scalding the teapot, put into it one quart of boiling water with two teaspoons of green tea. Strain,* without stirring, through a tea strainer into a pitcher. Let it stand till tea time and pour into decanters, leaving the sediment in the bottom of the pitcher. Fill the goblets with ice, put two teaspoons of granulated sugar in each, and pour the tea over the ice and sugar. A squeeze of lemon will make this delicious and healthful, as it will correct the astringent tendency.

To make the peach blend, the easiest thing to do is to boil 2 cups strong tea, mix it with frozen peach concentrate from your grocer's freezer, and then add tons of ice and a little sweetener. It makes the southern part of you want to go sit on a porch with a fan and sip tea.

FORMAL TEAS DON'T CONTAIN much humor. Like many rituals, they're not supposed to be funny. Many tea experts and connoisseurs aren't that funny and may even take offense if they discover you have bad tea habits. One of the tea experts I spoke with refused to answer any of my questions because she said I confused her with an herbalist, and she is an aromatic specialist. One of the more shocking revelations early on in the journey was how denigrating people who knew about tea could be toward those of us who are not as informed. If you sit down for a high tea, God forbid you eat a scone before the tea is poured; some people seem to think of that as mortal sin. If you go to a Chinese tea ceremony, don't even think about drinking because you are thirsty. I once asked for green tea in a tea shop and the man proceeded to give me a twenty-minute lecture on the variety of green teas, which made it impossible for him to select one without more information from me. I have added honey to tea and seen a British friend wince in pain at the vulgarity of the act.

Tea is just not funny. Humor can be added to tea only by the human touch. No one adds that touch better than southerners. We just throw in tons of sugar or alcohol or ice with pride. The saying is if you ask for tea in the North, it is hot; if you ask for it in the South, it is iced. The history of iced tea follows the same timeline as the manufacturing of ice in the 1860s South. Its popularity in the United States rose dramatically after the 1904 World's Fair in St. Louis, where it was served by Richard Blechynden, the Commissioner of Tea for India. Blechynden, an Englishman, had samples of hot tea for fairgoers. Due to the unseasonably hot day, people were only interested in cold beverages. Thinking quickly, he added ice to the tea, and the crowd loved it. There are iced teas dating back to the early 1800s, so Mr. Blechynden certainly didn't invent iced tea, but his quick thinking made it popular.

If you want to understand sweet tea, drink tea in Tennessee. I went on a weekend trip to Pigeon Forge, Tennessee, not too long ago to get a taste for the sweetness of life with my youngest son, Moses. It is the land of arcades, buffets, and dollar stores, and there is enough Tennessee in me that I can appreciate a good southern tourist attraction. I grew up going to the Opryland theme park before it turned into a mall. We rode old cars called Tin Lizzies and wandered for hours on a season pass; my mom used the amusement park like a day care center for middle schoolers. I remember a log ride and a whole area dedicated to the 1950s where workers wore ponytails and poodle skirts that I coveted. I like a carnival atmosphere and the idea of bargain entertainment, but even for a veteran fan of theme parks and southern tacky tourism, Pigeon Forge is surreal.

The huge six-lane strip called Pigeon Forge is carved into the foothills of the Great Smoky Mountains. The entertainment advertised along the road includes a history of the children who died in the *Titanic*, a Hatfield-and-McCoys log-rolling show, and a Chinese dance troupe from Cirque de Chine! Go-kart racing and putt-putt courses line the highway on both sides, crowding around hotels like the one I stayed in called Willow Brook Lodge (which has neither willows nor brooks). You could see the silhouette of the beautiful blue Smoky Mountains behind the neon signs advertising the Indian store, the pawnshop, and our destination: indoor skydiving.

We had traveled to Pigeon Forge for one reason: my wild love for my twelve-year-old son, whose dream was to try indoor skydiving. I drove the four hours and holed up in the hotel across the street from the facility. I was so nervous my safety goggles fogged before I started. I tried to pay attention as the instructor went through the hand signals and demonstrated how to tuck and roll when we fall out of the air tunnel. One of the sweet, unforgettable moments was watching my son take multiple dives. We left the adventure thirsty, probably because our mouths had been agape in 150-mile-an-hour winds. We hunted for a local shop that offered coffee and hot teas. But Pigeon Forge is strictly a coffee and sweet iced tea town. No green tea could be found except for the cans of sweet green tea offered in convenience stores by huge tea companies.

I once asked a tea expert which part of the world those large tea companies get their tea from, and he said, "The floor." Except for the Charleston Tea Plantation in South Carolina, all commercial tea is grown overseas and is hand-picked. Tea distributors make deals with large processing companies to take the tea after it's been picked through once.

They gather the bits of tea left and make the tea we mix with reconstituted lemon, artificial sweetener, and fructose to make instant iced tea. These seemed like perfect ingredients for the Pigeon Forge landscape: flashy packaging that leaves your mouth pursed from all the sugar. We left Pigeon Forge laughing at the joy of indulging in prepackaged amusement and overly sweet tea. It was good for a couple days not to have to be serious about tea and culture. It was a relief to gulp down a gallon of tea just because you feel thirsty. I don't want my tea or religion to be taken so seriously all the time. Sometimes I like to pray aloud without feeling someone is judging the words or to offer a sermon with some self-deprecating humor without anyone being offended. I want to share jokes with people I worship with and to live out what I believe in the midst of enjoying a day of work. I want to sit and laugh with everyone at Thistle Farms, not just weep for all the women still on the streets or for the fact that we are still short on skills and money. All of us need some levity to get to the perfect blend.

Another offshoot of sweet tea and the South is sun-brewed tea. I had always heard about brewing tea under the sun. I love the idea of it, and God knows it's been hot enough to fry an egg on the street here in Nashville. Literally. I have seen stories in the paper about people even frying eggs on the hoods of their cars. Setting out a gallon of water in a clear jug with tea bags floating in it gave me time to fret while my tea brewed. Beyond the laughter there was some real trepidation about the possibility that the café wouldn't move ahead. As I watched the water slowly turn into long, muddy brown streaks as the tea drained from the bags, I felt myself losing hope that the café would open, because of the lack of funds at Thistle Farms and the rapidly increasing costs of trying to renovate the space. In the past month we learned that the new heating, cooling, and electrical systems were going to cost about forty thousand more than we had hoped, and we had not had a single donation in a month. Furthermore, of the people volunteering, no one had ever built or run a café, and the learning curve is so steep I felt a bit of altitude sickness. This must be the hallowed ground where dreams go to die. They seep out and fade as slowly as the tea tannins into the water. They lose their luster under the eye of the sun, and we find ourselves reconciling with lost hope and trying to make the best of the reality that, either way, it probably couldn't matter that much. But as the tea continued to darken the water, I felt like turning it to a salty blend with my tears. I didn't know if the café would open, honestly. I thought if I told people it just may not happen, it would finally be revealed that I'm not capable enough. It scares me to think about failing. I saw the murky fear of failure in the sun-tanned water on my porch. I see it like a clear aura. What holds us all back in pursuing dreams and kicks our soul's ass is fear. My fear is not that I will be poor or fail but that others will see me as poor and a failure.

When fear takes precedence in our lives, whether due to real or imagined forces, practicing the way of tea helps us walk into a more loving, compassionate, and sweeter place. It is a decision we make to sweeten the cup we have been given. I was going to need to sweeten this sun tea brewing. It had been steeping for too long and it was going to be a bitter brew. In the story of the Jews wandering in the desert, they are given plain manna and water to quench their hunger and thirst. They murmur and complain, but they still drink it down, and it sustains them. Whether this café opened or not wasn't the issue. The issue was to keep drinking the cup I have been given faithfully. I am unworthy; we are all unworthy of the dreams we have been given and of the cup we have before us. It may not be the dream we would have chosen or the cup we would have picked, but it's ours to hold and drink from and then pour out for others. This is where the tea bag meets the water in the journey of discipleship. This is how we know we are loved.

What makes the tea of life sweet for me is the freedom to act on what I believe. It is so sweet to have a dream of a community and then to find a space and a group of people who offer one another the resources to act on that dream. The cup we have been given is sweetened with prayer and also with walks in the woods that let dreams steep among old oaks and ancient rocks. I had a dream not too long ago that I swam in the ocean with unbelievable freedom among secret and silent reefs. I awoke feeling like the sweetness of the dream was the freedom I felt to just swim. Whether we are hovering four feet above a huge skydiving fan or dreaming of going to the depths of the sea, freedom to live in our ideals of love has got to be the sweetest gift of all.

The cup we have been given is always sweetened when

we ground ourselves in gratitude. One of the most recent residents of Magdalene came and asked me to think about her when we started the hiring process. She sat in our meditation circle at Thistle Farms in the morning and began by saying to everyone that she was grateful to be there and be in the circle. I watched her in awe and tried to imagine the spiritual depth it took for her to come to gratitude. She was raped as a child, spent her teens on the streets addicted and trafficked, and followed up with spending her twenties in prison. She spoke about gratitude with a rich sweetness I can only pray to possess someday. She was sipping a sweet brew steeped in knowledge that few people in the world can fathom. She is accepting this cup so she can find a way to drink it in peace and then offer it to others. I toast her as my teacher as I sip the sun-brewed tea I made. I need reminding almost on a weekly basis that gratitude is the beating of a healthy heart. When I am frustrated by committees, I take a sip of tea and remember the gift of time that everyone on the committee is offering in order to see the vision of a café come to life. When I see colleagues' careers soaring and I'm wondering if I should have been more successful, I take a sip of tea and remember all the merriment and joy I have known from this path. When I worry about money or my kids growing and leaving home, I take another sip of tea and remember how everything I have ever needed has been there. When any of us find a way to move from fear to gratitude, life has been sweetened and love has been restored to our thoughts.

No clearer image depicts the feeling of gratitude after

being lost than that of the lost sheep described in the Gospels. When we have wandered by choice or circumstances to a place where we are alone, the story of the lost sheep reminds us that no one is outside of love's embrace. The lost sheep calls us in faith. When we encounter a woman on the streets who has been victimized before she could even identify where she lived on a map, we don't give up but find a way to welcome her home. Idealism says there is no one on all of God's green earth who is hopeless, even if it feels that way. The lost sheep is a call to humility. There is nothing more humbling than to realize we are lost and need some help. In humility, we can accept help from others and face insurmountable obstacles in the justice, education, or penal systems working on behalf of the marginalized. While we are aware of our limitations in strength and resources, in community we find solace and remember that we never have to abandon anyone on the road to hope. And finally, humility is a call to gratitude. Whether searching for another lost sheep or feeling lost, we remember that even here we are not abandoned. Instead, even in our most desolate times, there is a path that calls us home with grateful hearts. Grateful hearts are the recipe to make our cup sweet. Gratitude is the sweet knowledge that we have been forgiven and loved perfectly and completely and we can find our way back to community.

One example of how we can walk a path toward gratitude comes from one of the oldest gardens in the United States, the Morikami Japanese gardens in Delray Beach, Florida. Beyond the wonder of its rich flora, the garden features a collection of bonsai, some of which are more than four hundred years old. The founder of the gardens was an immigrant from Japan in the 1920s who lived so others could enjoy the path. He slowly purchased, donated, and cultivated the land for preservation in forty- to fifty-acre lots. As you walk this quiet and beautiful path, you can feel gratitude rise in you as you realize what a gift it all is. George Morikami could have saved his money and built a mansion and fenced the whole space just for himself. But he gave it to the community so that we can walk the way of tea and feel gratitude for the beauty of the earth and the generosity of our fellow walkers.

The Japanese gardens carved out a place of peace and gratitude from a distant land. It's the same kind of generous spirit that enables a community to come together and hammer out the details of a dream that moves us closer to justice and tea. The sweetest paths are those that are carved for others to walk. Paths that make it possible for people like Dorris to find her way to the beach and dip her toes in the ocean. I'm grateful for the sweet tea on the way that keeps our spirit light and full of gratitude.

*Chapter Seven*

# THE PARADISE OF TEA

## Darjeeling

All Darjeeling tea comes from India, specifically the district of Darjeeling in the province of West Bengal, India. The tea gardens in this region have become so famous that they're now a popular tourist destination where people come to see and savor. Many consider Darjeeling the champagne of teas. While it's usually sold as a black tea, you can also find it available as a semi-oxidized oolong tea.

An important step in serving Darjeeling and other fine teas is the art of scalding the pot. Before you steep tea, pour some of the boiling water from the kettle into the teapot, swirl it around, and pour it out. This ensures a clean, hot teapot. The best infuser for Darjeeling is a simple stainless steel basket that allows the leaves to plump up and move freely, releasing all the flavors.

A DREAMY ISLAND NEAR NAPLES, Florida, seems like a close approximation of what paradise must be like, so I jumped at the chance to go there to speak at a retreat. I headed there with an exotic tea I had never tasted before, but according to the seller, it tasted close to perfection. On the first morning the beach was quiet, and the sun was greeting the day with new life over a sparkling ocean with pelicans dive-fishing and an osprey making a broad sweep. As I was crossing the boardwalk, I could see sweet little sandpipers scampering on the sand like a flash mob that all received the same text. What I couldn't understand was why I was completely alone in this paradise.

But as soon as I stepped onto the beach with my tea in hand, the stench was almost overpowering. The tide was going out and where the high tide usually leaves a spattering of shells and seaweed, there were tons of dead fish. I mean *tons*. There were blowfish, grouper, and manta rays, along with smaller baitfish, too many to number. I kept walking, wondering what had happened to all these fish and this beautiful beach. About another mile down, I ran into a uniformed biologist who worked for the state who explained to me the die-off was from a red tide. Red tide is an algae bloom, which the scientist explained came from fertilizers that get into the brackish water. As the red tide enters the bay and mixes with the salt water, it becomes a toxic mixture. Paradise on that beach was just an illusion, and the truth of how broken and hurting the world can be was visible in the huge mounds of dead fish and seaweed. This was a moment when the curtain was pulled back, and I faced a truth I hadn't considered before. I had never thought about red tides or how lawn chemicals mix with seawater. It was sad and sobering to see how quickly and quietly a paradise can sour. As I kept walking to learn the lessons of this illusion, I kept my tea close to breathe in its aroma. Paradise is surely an idea of better times and better places, but maybe it is a part of the way of tea and justice, too.

My friend John Prine writes about paradise in one of his songs and says that when he dies and floats away, he will be about halfway to heaven, and paradise will still be waiting just a few miles down the road. Many of us carry that feeling with us most of our lives—that paradise is about five miles away from wherever we are. Paradise is just yonder in the sweet by-and-by and it's something coming our way. Humanity has always thought that way. If one thing or another would change, then we would be happy in the illusion we call paradise. We can't imagine that in the midst of our trouble and shortfalls, paradise is already here. If we define paradise as life with God, then wherever we are, we can find paradise. Paradise is almost impossible to see or feel most of the time, though. In the Gospel story about Jesus walking with the disciples James and John, He is trying to help them grasp this concept of paradise.

In the tenth chapter of Mark, Jesus is walking to Jerusalem

with the disciples as He predicts His death for a third time. He uses James's and John's misconceptions about paradise as a way to talk about living within the bounds of love. They imagine a heavenly banquet where Jesus presides, where they feast on His right and left. They are walking with Jesus and still imagining that paradise is somewhere else. Paradise was right there, and they couldn't see it because of the brokenness around them and their own fears. Jesus then explains what it is to have a life with Him and teaches them about the three things needed to live in paradise.

Laying hold of paradise takes a willingness to suffer for the sake of love. We have to be willing to allow our lives to be about redemptive suffering to understand the profound depth of living in the presence of eternal love. We also have to be willing to let go of what we claim is ours to see the magnitude of the paradise Jesus offers us. The third aspect of being able to live in paradise now, Jesus explains to James and John, is a willingness to live without judgment. No one can decide who gets to reside there; it is not even Jesus' prerogative to judge. All we can do is love. There is no true paradise with judgment, ranking, or power. Living in paradise means looking for every opportunity to serve. When we live a life full of service in love, we are there already. In the beautiful hills of Darjeeling, where some of the lushest gardens for tea are tended and where some people eke out a life on subsistence wages, paradise can be found. It's found in loving families and committed communities trying to work toward a more just system. In places such as Darjeeling, paradise rises with the sun in hills with pleated colors and spins out to the world like a dervish in midprayer. When we see that the place where we are holds both beauty and devastation, we can find paradise. Our breath catches or our eyes water as we see the world washed in love. That's when we can lift our eyes to the heavens and hear our calling on the wind. I am right where I need to be, drinking this tea along the ghost-town coast in Florida. This may be as close as I get to paradise. From this place I can sip tea like communion. The red tide is passing and I am walking its wake. When we are gifted with eyes that can contemplate the universe, it is a short walk to feeling like we are surrounded by holiness.

I recently read about the Tea Board of India, a large alliance of tea growers and traders who determine the rights of trading and naming tea. A ten-year battle has been fought over the name "Darjeeling tea," because of how the name is used in branding. The board has given growers of Darjeeling tea the same rights as growers of some wines. People can no longer buy blended tea called Darjeeling. The Darjeeling tea makers have waited a decade for this victory. If they kept up their will to keep fighting for the rights of their tea, surely we can keep going and working to see the café come to life. We have spent many hours in our work at Thistle Farms feeling frustrated by the busy pace, the chaotic nature of more than fifty folks in recovery trying to work together and trying to accommodate all the volunteers' needs. Sometimes it's almost like we can feel the temperature rise in the room. It is not unheard of to have to leave a meeting to go to another part of the facility because you can hear voices rising and I wonder if this time the kettle will blow. We are all working in a new area and trying to grow a company that lives the ideals of love. It is like birthing: hard and miraculous. Sometimes when I start to hatch an exit plan to escape, I think about Carole, who is a full-time volunteer in her seventies who works to plan events. She practices her contemplative prayer life, even in the midst of that stress. She has laid hold of one of the great secrets of living in paradise.

One summer day not too long ago in the middle of a sales drought, the manufacturing department started complaining that we needed more raw materials. But we also needed money from new sales to purchase them. We were told by some of our economic advisors that it might be better to put the whole capital campaign to build the café on hold. I went upstairs frustrated and stressed, only to find Carole quietly working at her desk with an aura of peace surrounding her that was powerful enough to calm even me down. She loves creating a paradise in the midst of a storm, and it rubs off on others. Carole stirs a hunger in me for more of paradise.

There may be no better way to get there than through the path of deep silence. Silence is a great environment in which to encounter God and ourselves. Silence is the deep presence of truth, not the absence of words. The words "nausea" and "noise" come from the same root, and one of the greatest sicknesses is all the noise that fills our world and our heads. Noise keeps heaven at bay. Seeing Carole working silently and at peace, I realized I was watching someone who had firmly set herself in heaven while we wailed. I thought everything was falling apart, but she was in communion with the spirit. We don't get to paradise by stressing or being pulled into a vortex of chaos. We get there by heading in the direction of silence and toward our interior castles.

St. Teresa of Avila wrote about the seven mansions that live within us in her prayerful autobiography, *Interior Castle*[14]. The path to this interior castle is the path of prayer, no matter how much we struggle to maintain a life of prayer. When we find the way inside our souls, we remember that paradise lives within us. It may be hard to find due to the stench of rotting fish on a beach or broken dreams that we counted on, but it is there for the seeking. This is it. This is paradise, and from this vantage point, we can see the paradises that we missed.

In 1908, Marcel Proust described with poetic imagery how tea creates paradise. He was in his apartment and still shivering from a late-night walk when tea was brought to him. "When he idly dipped in it a finger of dry toast and raised the sodden mixture to his lips, he was overwhelmed once more by the mysterious joy which marked the onset of unconscious memory." He caught the scent of geraniums and was carried back to his childhood. This tea epiphany led to his writing *A la recherché du temps perdu* (*In Search of Lost Time*).[15] The memory of tea is powerful, like the image of paradise itself. Tea can carry us around time without the constraints of a timeline. It can carry us back to childhood, to its roots in China, or even to a paradise we only dream of. A cup of tea can be the vehicle to carry us, wherever we are, right to where we need to be. It can bring us to a place of peace no matter where we find ourselves.

Tea has been a companion to poets and a muse for dreamers since the first person thought of the idea of paradise. In *The Wind and the Willows*, Toad has tea with a girl. "Toad sat up on end once more, dried his eyes, sipped his tea and munched his toast, and soon began talking freely about himself, and the house he lived in, and his doings there, and how important he was."[16] Of course a fanciful toad wanting to woo a beautiful girl to help him escape his fate would turn to tea to create a vision of paradise. Even toads can dream of being princes through the gift of tea.

There is a reference to the teapot (the "billy boiling") in one of the best-known folk songs, called "Waltzing Matilda," a dreamy rendition of a harsh farming life in Australia. The song describes a wanderer carrying a matilda, or bag, who sets up camp under the shade of a tree: "And he sang as he looked at his old billy boiling, / Who'll come a-waltzing Matilda with me?"

Authors and poets can hear the pot of boiling water calling like a siren to delve into their imagined paradises, lost and found. Tea becomes a means for toads to escape and for homeless wanderers to find a moment's peace. It is a path of hope for all of us that we can dream of better times and live better in the time we have.

In all of the spaces and places of life, tea helps us remember that the journey of walking toward paradise is remembering how we were walking in paradise all along. We are walking in paradise even through the longest nights and through the valleys of the shadow of death. Like St. Teresa and St. Julian before us, we can find the gift of paradise as close as our next breath when we remember that even that breath is a gift from our loving God. But it is hard to keep visions close and remember we are walking with the holy.

Even with a perfect cup of tea, there are times as we go through the valleys that it feels as if visions become blurry and distant. We feel so far away from abiding in paradise we almost can't imagine it. During these months of planning the café venture, paradise feels like it's too far to reach. There are so many pieces and so little time that we need to postpone the opening. I write of peace, yet the thought of opening this café made me feel frantic. I had to leave a meeting just the other day to rush to the hospital to give last rites to a dying woman not too much older than me. As I pulled up to the hospital parking lot, a hawk was perched on the church across the way and another was circling overhead. The scene was a haunting gift. *There is no need to get frantic,* I saw the hawks say as clearly as a banner behind a prop plane flying on the shoreline. Being frantic just blurs visions and tempts us to think that paradise is a mirage. Believing that we have been left out of paradise is reinforced by old fears and the criticism of others. This day is a gift, and there damn well might not be another one. Tomorrow may be the day another pastor is called to say prayers over me. Our hope in faith is to live in the eternal paradise and not wait. Not wait until the café is built, or the kids are bigger, or we aren't in debt, or we are in love. This is the day that we have been given to live in our dreams, no matter how distant or blurry those dreams are.

I met with a businessman who told me to put on my tough skin as I poured him a cup of hot water over a rich Kenyan black tea bag in a china cup I had received from Scotland. I told him I didn't own that skin and it would be better if he started and ended on a positive note, which to his credit he did. But the middle, oh the middle, the middle is where he questioned whether any of this venture of Thistle Farms and the café was sustainable. He asked me if, because Thistle Farms asks for money every year, we were ready to open a new business while this one was still in need. He made some good points, but I think he missed the real one.

We are not serving tea to strangers just because we love tea. We are serving tea because we love women, and the way to continue loving women is to serve tea. As we were talking, I realized that he never took the tea bag out of his cup, and the tea was so dark it looked like espresso and was probably horribly bitter. So after I explained the financial workings of my dream, I told him the story of a woman in the community who was raped by a relative for many years, trafficked, and along the way was arrested more than a hundred times. After three years of her sobriety, today her daughter and six-month-old grandbaby are living with her and healing together. The outcome for the grandbaby has dramatically shifted, and because the child will grow up safe and secure, we as a community called Nashville are more sustainable. I couldn't tell if he captured a glimpse of our dream of paradise out of the harsh reality of life, but he took another sip of his sad cup of tea before he left. I wonder sometimes if paradise might even be harder to see from the vantage point of great wealth and power.

Historically, people have paid high premiums for fine tea, for the sweet dream of power and success it offers. Tea has always been seen as a valuable commodity in the West, and we lose sight of the precious pearl it offers us to heal and be at peace as people race to trade and gain wealth from it. I don't want to focus on the dream of paradise sold by tea traders. I want us all to remember how tea led us to the precious pearls on this earth, as described in the Gospel. These precious pearls are the nuggets of truth that are worth so much that people sell their land to buy them. They are elusive and instructive. They make us pay attention to every detail and nuance in the life of the tea. They make us want to craft the vessel that will hold it and the fine linen to place underneath it. They call us to our best and make us yearn to help the women serving it. It is not just the way of tea that is precious; it is the women in all their stunning blessedness serving it. The paradise of tea lies in its ability to help us find our way to the altars of truth.

As stated in Isaiah 43:1–7: "But now thus says the Lord, he who created you, O Jacob, he who formed you, O Israel: Do not fear, for I have redeemed you; I have called you by name, you are mine. When you pass through the waters, I will be with you; and through the rivers, they shall not overwhelm you; when you walk through fire you shall not be burned, and the flame shall not consume you. For I am the Lord your God, the Holy One of Israel, your Savior. I give Egypt as your ransom, Ethiopia and Seba in exchange for you. Because you are precious in my sight, and honored, and I love you, I give people in return for you, nations in exchange for your life. Do not fear, for I am with you."

I first read this passage at sixteen years old. I was on a search for meaning in faith and tried to reconcile that desire with the exilic experience of high school. I loved this passage so much I carved "I have called you by name, you are mine" into a piece of wood and shellacked it. Our lives are the precious pearl nurtured by the gifts of creation like tea or oil or food. When we honor one another as beloved, put out our good cups, lay our nice clothes, stir toward our hearts, and take time to offer compassion, it's easier to remember how everyone is a precious pearl. Discovering the precious pearl in us feels like paradise on earth.

When we see the precious pearl within another person, we take on the pain of loving and bear the burden of grief. So it is that in discovering paradise, we are willing to bear the cost of loving eternally in temporal time. Living in paradise means we are willing to pay the cost of buying the field that held the precious pearl. Loving one another is the joy that makes us want to work toward justice and seek the beauty of this world. There is no tea that can take away the sting of death or the cost of loving. There is simply the renewed strength to live closer to our ideals of paradise. It is amazing how quickly everything but love returns to dust. The hours spent organizing don't keep the chaos at bay; the lawn goes to seed quickly after years of tending.

Seeing death blurs our vision, making us nearsighted so that our weeping eyes can't see the forest for the beautiful falling oak. Seeing love illuminates our vision so that not only can we see the forest holding the tree, but we can glimpse the eternal sky under which it grew. Tea is the leaf that helps me see the paradise and promise of the heavens. If you listen closely, you can hear paradise calling as tea whistles for us to come. It beckons us like an old friend to sit with our dreams and memories and wonder.

Paradise is within reach when we surrender to love without judgment and to service to others. We surrender to love and service not so we can get to paradise but in gratitude for the truth that we are already there. We are walking with Jesus down a road, heading to Jerusalem, and it may never get better than this moment. Tea is a companion to awaken us to the truth that wherever we are, paradise is found. As we hold a steamy cup close to our hearts, we're reminded of the presence of hope and paradise in our midst.

*Chapter Eight*

# MEDICINAL TEA

## Recipe for Throat-Coat Tea

One of the great joys of the journey of tea is to make your own blends of loose-leaf tea mixed with herbs and seeds known for their healing qualities. It is not hard to do and can be a beautiful gift. I learned about a great blend for throat-coat tea that includes black tea, dried lemon rind, licorice, and a bit of slippery elm bark that soothes your throat. You can add a pinch of orange rind or a stick of cinnamon bark to bring an added layer to the flavor to the tea. Purchase these ingredients at a local natural food or health store or online.

Mix 2 teaspoons black tea with ¼ teaspoon lemon rind, ⅛ teaspoon licorice, and ⅛ teaspoon elm bark. Place the ingredients in an empty tea bag. Yield is 2 cups tea. Feel free to add honey to the warm water after the tea bag has steeped for 3 to 5 minutes.

I WOKE UP WITH THAT familiar feeling of a scratch in the back of my throat. I never like that eerie sense that I've caught something somewhere. Whatever that something might be, we must squelch it before it makes a nest in our bodies and becomes a full-blown cold or infection. The medicinal teas that line my windowsill are my go-to on mornings like this. It was still dark as I crept into the kitchen to find the Eastern blend of herbs and green tea designed to coat my throat. The first healing notion came when I realized that my cup runneth over, literally. It was so dark, I couldn't see the water line and poured hot water all over the counter. The old-school herbal teas ward off all kinds of bad things like aches, pains, and itchy throats. I can drink them and imagine my immune system kicking in and my body flushing out every bad germ as the tea coats me with a loving feeling. I was going to sip tea all day and get ready to feel the scratchiness in my throat and heart being soothed with each kind cup.

These are the kind of healing teas that I hope we serve in the café. I want our teas to heal the mind, body, soul, spirit, and heart. These kinds of teas don't just have medicinal qualities to heal physical discomfort; they also heal human inequality. When we began Magdalene, we thought helping to heal five women took a large group. Looking back, we can see that it took a whole community. We will pour out tea and feel a healing power in the brew and in the love with which it is served. We want to serve teas that nourish us and the women who harvest them. But as I sip the healing tea, I wonder if the café itself isn't making me feel a little sick—especially our recent meeting with the contractors. Because our budget is under theirs by a hundred thousand dollars, they believe all we can do is leave things like demolition, flooring, painting, interiors, lights, and countertops to volunteers. Once again, it feels as if our small group is being asked to conduct an orchestra without knowing how to read music. It wasn't the contractors' fault or our fault; it was just that the reality of the gap between what we hoped to build and what we can afford to build is vast. Right now it's as wide as the Mississippi. Because we need to cross it soon, we need either to find a boat or to make friends with some bridge builders.

All we could do after the meeting was make adjustments, figure out what skill sets we needed, and trust that the rest of the money will come. During the meeting, the contractors waived parts of their own fees, called friends to donate a few hours, and promised they would continue to reduce costs as they worked through the project with us. Despite our capable and beautiful team doing the footwork, the to-do list and budgetary needs continued to pile up. When thoughts of being overwhelmed enter our unimaginably busy lives, a scratchy throat is not a bad wake-up call.

Tea is a whistle calling us to pay attention to our bodies. Tea whistles sound like old church bells that take the time to ring out each hour. The pot calls, and we know a respite from the stress and pace of the busyness of this world is before us. In fantasy and fact, tea calls us to the table to sit and reflect and delve deeper into our hearts. The healing quality of tea, therefore, begins before we ever take a sip. The act of preparing and anticipating a hot cup of tea can begin the process of healing us from the outside forces that want to curb our ability to sit in peace and our desire to dream without judgment. Like no other drink on the planet, tea invites us to stop and rest our weary souls. I wonder if Jesus would have liked to raise a cup of tea when He promised His disciples that His yoke is easy and His burden light. Tea would have been the perfect drink for that lesson. We can bear the injustices in the world and the stress of trying to live well when we sit with fellow travelers and prepare tea for one another. We are just beginning to wake up to the healing elements of tea in the United States. While Native Americans have mixed tinctures of herbs for healing, it wasn't until the Eastern traditions got traction in our open markets that people started craving green tea and the traditional blends of herbs.

One way to experience the medicinal gift of tea is to sit at a tea party and watch the healing that unfolds in the stories and sharing offered by the guests. Tea parties can be simple or fancy, and can offer intimacy along with scones. Wherever and however tea is prepared and offered, an invitation to tea conjures up images of lovely place settings, linens, friends, and discussion deeper than the beverage. Tea gatherings are becoming an endangered, rare gift in the United States that connects us, honors the people we love, heals the broken, and offers rest to the weary. The twenty-first-century's Tea Party political group in America is in some ways the antithesis of the inclusivity and communal atmosphere called for in an old-school tea party. The political group's verbiage condemning compromise and the notion of the common good devalues the beauty of a tea party that celebrates varied opinions and stories to create a new vision for all.

One of the fanciest tea parties I've ever been to took place in Greenwich, Connecticut. It was given in honor of Thistle Stop Café's desire to collect teacups from around the world. The setting looked like an English country estate at 4:00 PM, or at least how I imagine country estates look on afternoons. The entire tea service was silver, and the cup and linens were of the finest quality. The guests were dressed without an unwanted wrinkle or stray hair. The host held the party in the fellowship hall of Christ Church, and women were invited to bring an old teacup or linen to donate to the café and share their story. It was beautiful, healing, and lavish. Women from all political parties and representing several countries and generations shared their hope in the story of the cup they offered to the café. As each woman stood and told the story of the cup she brought, we sipped tea, laughed, and cried at the resurrected memories of dead ancestors and the heroic tales of our mothers. Tea transformed into a balm for hearts that needed hope.

I felt like I was in the story of the toad and the girl in 1908 or sitting in a scene from *Little Women*. The age range of the women attending was between forty and ninety-eight. The oldest woman brought a tea saucer that came from Japan during World War II, when Japanese Americans were put into internment camps. She showed us the marking on the bottom of the plate and explained how the United States had banned imports from Japan at the time. But this piece, with a Japanese stamp, was brought in by a friend. The next woman, who had a thick Russian accent, brought a piece that belonged to a friend who had been a refugee. The cup was chipped, but she had stored it for years. Now she wanted to pass it along to the survivors of the streets. One of the many ways tea brings healing is by challenging us to examine our past and embrace a new future. There was a cup donated by a woman who was trapped in a violent marriage. She felt stuck, thinking that somehow it was all her fault.

An image came to her in a dream from which she woke with a start to a voice saying "Your cup is empty." She offered her cup to the café endeavor with the truth that we can refill cups with a spirit that revives, not leaves us isolated and lost. The healing offered to us by tea and the cups that hold it is as unique as the sicknesses and burdens we bear.

One story we received after the tea party embodies much of what our hopes for healing in the café look like. This woman didn't own any china or teacups, but she wanted to make a donation to the Thistle Stop Café. She went off to buy a cup at the kind of shop that would have something she could afford. The first cup she saw was beautiful and within her budget. At the counter, she shared the story behind her purchase with the store owner. "But it doesn't have a handle," he protested. "Are you sure you still want it?" "Yes," she said; "it is beautiful." She then explained that she left the shop grasping her new purchase firmly. She wondered why the china cup was made the way it was. The handle-less cup became a symbol for her to recognize how a beautiful difference can draw us in. We are made in the Potter's hands, just like teacups, and none is exactly the same as another. To take the comparison just a step further, every person on earth has a genetic code that shares the same alphabet; we all have commonalities that make us like a beautiful set of vastly different teacups. We each have unique desires and hopes, but we share a common need for healing and nourishment.

Another story shared was an example of the joy that rises from the ashes of grief and how a cup can hold them both. A dear friend had lost her mother. She asked another friend to take a tiny bouquet of red roses in her mother's special china teacup to church the next Sunday, so that worshippers could enjoy the beautiful funeral flowers during the service. Walking toward the church, the friend slipped on the ice and the cup shattered. She searched for a substitute, found the closest match she could at a nearby store, and planned to tell the grieving daughter after the service.

When the daughter sat down to worship, she noticed it was someone else's cup holding the roses. The friend was forced to come clean about the switch. They laughed as the daughter listened to her friend explain her duplicitous efforts. The women decided the best place for the cup was at the Thistle Stop Café, because the women of Magdalene know that good things—like laughter and love—can come out of brokenness. Sometimes the brokenness itself allows us to let go of what we would hold on to forever if given the choice. If her mother's cup had never broken, she may never have been able to let the precious cup go so that a whole community could hear her story and she could find a glimpse of healing.

The most tender cup of healing I received over the course of collecting cups came from my sister. After my mother died in 1997, my sister was given Mom's thistle pattern tea set. The set was sadly depleted by decades of use and consisted only of several plates, the top to the sugar bowl, the creamer, and one single teacup and saucer. My sister placed the pieces on the shelf of her kitchen where we paid tribute to it with sweet compliments when we were at her house visiting. After we announced that we wanted to collect cups, my sister wrapped the very last teacup and saucer that my mom left and said that she thought Mom would want it to be in the café. I never would have dreamed of asking my sister for that cup, but it is a great gift to the healing hope that we want emanating from that space.

It is so sad to let go of relics of those we love, but doing so breathes new life into their memories and stories. There was nothing pretentious about the tea party in Greenwich and the ten other tea parties given in honor of the café. All the gatherings did was make us want to start a movement of flash tea parties, where communities anywhere and anytime can gather and share stories and cups and feel that we were getting fortified by the love and tea. The first tea party in Greenwich was a huge gift to us at Thistle Farms. We love the notion that tea can be generous. It can be so generous that cups multiply before your eyes as people come to share a sip of hope.

We should pour tea out for each other like prayers for healing and comfort. We should share our stories and celebrate lives well lived. We should toast with tea and not let life pass us by. All the stories of tea and all the healing present give me the energy I need to keep going, whether my throat feels scratchy or not. I want to serve tea to as many people as possible and drink until it is gone. I pray that we get another thousand teacups and stories so that we are sated in a healing tea party that holds people we never even knew but get to share a cup with.

As a thousand people gathered in our last fundraiser for the café, a woman I met the night before lingered in my mind. Two days ago, this twenty-five-year-old arrived on the doorstep of Magdalene off a Greyhound bus. She had been in prison for eighteen months. She said she had been writing Magdalene for a year from inside the prison walls in Arkansas, hoping to find her way home. She looked like a stray, and I wondered if Magdalene could ever become her home or if she could ever find her voice. The previous night was the rehearsal for the annual fundraising event for Thistle Farms and her first outing. We were all gathered and singing "I Shall Be Released." She sang with her arms open wide and head thrown back that she "sees her light come shining." I take in another warm taste and pray the night to go well so we can keep it all going.

At the end of the event, I learned about the newest volunteer to sign on to the café. James Worsham is a designer who specializes in taking teacups and combining them with found objects and old wood to create sculptures. It was a divine gift that one of the few teacup designers in the world had come our way. He could take all the beautiful healing

122

stories in the cups and create pieces of art that would make their light shine for others. When we offer our stories, the right people are there to write the next chapter.

## Peggy's Story for the Café

*Having admired the Magdalene and Thistle Farms programs for years, I decided to get involved in 2012 when I heard that a café was in the works. I had spent several decades working with women in recovery from eating disorders, and I felt called to share my experience and hope with others. At the time, I thought the Thistle Stop Café might be a place where I could be of service to others, but what I would soon find out is that I had come home. While touring the proposed café building with my husband, I was inspired by Becca's vision of what could grow out of the space. I mentioned that I was a photographer, and Becca said, "Well, I just got out of a café meeting, and the only position we really need is a photographer." It felt like it was meant to be—a small sign to me. Little did I know, but my photography skills would also qualify me to paint walls, wash dishes, serve tea, listen to stories, laugh, and give many, many hugs.*

*The spiritual principles that guide the Magdalene programs have infused every step of my journey with the café. My first project was photographing the teacups donated from all over the world. I was struck by how such a small gesture—one person sending in a single teacup—created hope and energy. These cups were signs that there was a large family of support from across the world lending their prayers. From this first photography project, I witnessed how small changes can make a big difference, and I see this principle at work throughout the café—from how a smile from across the counter can turn a day around or how the life of a woman can be made better by a customer's choice to use the products made by the Magdalene women. There is a story in every cup, and I am grateful to be a small part of the healing transformations that take place in the cafe every day. I know that love heals.*

—Peggy Napier

One of the best gifts tea offers is its constant presence day in and day out. It is there during high-stress days and still shows up the next morning when it's all a memory. It is healing to have a daily presence that is there winter or summer, rain or shine, joy or grief. Our bodies long for healing teas like a deer longs for water. We hunger for a time and space that can't be sated by pills or words. We must create and till our interior garden. Tea can water that space and cultivate a rich plot of spirit. There is so much to be grateful for about tea. It is there when our throats are scratchy in the early morning hours, and we worry over health. Tea holds us up when we are shaky and gives us a constant presence to nurture our interior lives. Tea brings communities and volunteers together and offers a viable way for people to enter a community. Tea is the healing gift that can lift our spirits faster than it takes a kettle to come to a boil.

*Chapter Nine*

# A CUP OF UNDERSTANDING

## Ginseng Tea

People have used ginseng in their diets to support a healthy immune system and focus their minds. This is a great tea when you are hoping for more clarity and insight.

Mix ½ tablespoon green tea and ½ teaspoon dried ginseng together, place into a tea bag, and steep it in hot water for about 5 minutes. Drink it each morning for a week and see how the morning comes into focus and your spirit is revived.

OFTEN, THINGS FEEL DIFFERENT than you imagine they will. I had thought about visiting the Charleston Tea Plantation and was prepared to feel a bit of righteous indignation by injustices I assumed I would see. But experience leads to understanding if we keep a student's heart. When my friend Tara and I arrived, the smell of damp, thick air slowed our pace and opened our hearts. We walked beneath old live oaks draped in Spanish moss, which look like shawls for old bark that make aging gracefully appear easy. The first moment of revelation that things were different than I imagined came within minutes as deerflies swarmed and hovered in the swampy land surrounding pristine tea fields. Their bites are hard and give you the feeling you are in a Hitchcock movie as you hear increasing numbers flying like B1 bombers toward your vulnerable skin. Because the farm is organic, the flies thrive as the harvest begins in the middle of May. Before I arrived I might have criticized the farm for using chemicals, but as I walked through the field, I thought that if I had to work there, I might beg for pesticides to engage in chemical warfare against these killer flies.

The next revelation came as we stopped to visit with the workers walking between the rows picking weeds. They were naturalists, mostly male, and represented the great diversity and culture of America. One of the guys took a picture as Tara and I posed with tea plants, then another worker stopped what he was doing to patiently explain the varieties of *Camellia sinensis* growing and the new varieties being developed. The size and scope of the machinery were amazing. The entire place is harvested with a single machine the workers call the Green Giant, which they have used for thirty years. It cuts a few inches off the tea plants every twenty-five days for eight months out of the year. Replacement parts for the Green Giant take months to acquire. In my stereotypical thinking, I had assumed that the fields would be filled with immigrant women holding chemical tanks. Instead, an organic farm with fair hiring practices and care for the workforce greeted and humbled us.

The mechanized processing of the leaves was a bit disillusioning, though. The machines pulverized all the leaves and erased my romantic notion of wilting leaves with people separating leaf from stem. Instead, large magnetic belts and rollers and huge drying tumblers with long conveyor belts processed the tea. Traveling there and hearing the story and seeing the workers' attention to taste and varieties were a gift.

The biggest shock for me was the desire that rose within me to pick just a few of the million leaves off the plants. It wasn't really stealing, I reasoned; I just wanted to see if we could grow our own plants from cuttings. The managers of the estate told us the plant varieties were secret, and it would take five years to grow a plant to harvest, but I wanted some tea for myself. Walking through those fields and fantasizing for a moment about sneaking a tea plant out conjured up the image of the great tea spy, Robert Fortune, who stole thousands of plants from the interior of

China. He disguised himself with native dress and a long braid and spent years trying to bring samples out of China into England. My desire for this tea cowers in the secret colonial part of my heart, compelling me so that when I see a beautiful crop, I want to own the field. I don't want to just taste tea or learn from tea; somewhere within me I want to *own* tea.

The tea plantation is powerful and raw and lovely. Its surprising reality is a good reminder of how we need to understand before we judge what we don't know. Maybe that is why Jesus says that the most radical way to love is without judgment. We can't judge until we understand, and we still don't understand it all yet. We may never understand it until we are ready to transition to the other side of time. Maybe then we can glimpse how it all makes sense, how we have been traveling with unseen wisdom and been offered mercy by the gallons from people who chose not to judge us.

Heading back home from the tea estate and a speaking engagement on All Saints' Day was a bit stressful because I knew construction had to begin immediately if we were to open the café on time. The reality that we may have to move our opening date for the café was sinking in as I sipped ginseng tea on the kind of faith that is not a feeling but a practice I have come to rely on when feelings fail me. I must trust in the forces bigger than me. I don't understand what is happening or what will unfold. I don't have any more faith now than when I was twenty; the only difference is now I act on my faith more than on my doubts.

All Saints' Day is the day to celebrate the early martyrs

whose names we do not know. It is also the day that we celebrate all the people we have loved who have died, who are so numerous they could fill the sky with huge billows of clouds that can pour down rain like tears for all the love they hold. It is the day we celebrate the newest saints in this cloud.

We finally ended the trip and departed Philadelphia about thirty minutes before the airport was shut down as the winds picked up and Superstorm Sandy headed in. The rain was pelting and the wind was pushing the plane around while we picked up speed on the runway. As we started ascending into the thick mass of clouds, I was reminded that clouds hold heft and power. They carry the wind and rain and are a force unto themselves. During the bumpiest ride I have experienced, I felt peace. I started thinking about the cloud of witnesses being like those clouds. The spiritual clouds hold history, power, and a store of knowledge that moves us toward love. I love this day and thinking about all those who walked before us and are part of the saints, tea drinkers, and dreamers who move us to keep walking with courage and humility.

As I flew through the sky, I thought about sweet Jeanne Bodfish, who had helped us form Magdalene and Thistle Farms in the first few years of our existence and had died recently at the age of eighty-three. She was a great teacher and friend, fearless in the political arena and on her spiritual path. Jeanne was a powerful force. I can almost hear her lilting voice, see her legacy, and feel her in the stormy wind and rain. We are surrounded by saints pulling us onto holy ground, casting off all the baggage we carry and don't need and drawing us close to the truth of eternity. We are here in the midst of a mighty force of saints, here with God.

We are surrounded by saints, not as spectators but as forces of faith in our lives. We feel them as surely as the thick clouds surrounding a powerful storm. In the gale-force winds above a hurricane, it's possible to feel encompassed by the cloud of witnesses. The saints remind us that we are working toward ideals that have been pursued by millions before. When I am afraid or think that no one ever had such trials, I can count on the saints who had their own fears and anxieties to set me free from the snare of fear.

When we draw on the wisdom, courage, and energy of the cloud of witnesses, it is possible for us to be carried with that cloud to a higher ground where we are capable of loving one another, God, and ourselves like the saints before us. It is possible that we can keep going with our visions, even with no map on a starless night. We can hold fast to our dreams, big and small, and feel love pulling us toward this eternal present. I wish I could have stayed above the storm and held fast to that powerful feeling of faith. But as we landed, I knew I was ready, come hell or high water, to keep trying to see the café and the way of tea come to life.

Understanding comes from learning about what is around us, like the tea estate, and from weathering storms. When you study the saints and soar through the clouds, the greatest glimpse of truth to glean is that we are truly free. In the midst of the storm and on the ground, it feels like we are trapped and unable to see the big picture. But instead, we are free to live our lives and live our dreams. Freedom then becomes a means of finding understanding.

In Paul's letter to the Galatians, written around AD 58, he questions those who are trying to judge if he was a true disciple because he is not abiding by the common practices of his day. This letter is a defense in which Paul helps the Galatians see the freedom in faith that unbinds us from the burden of judgment. This letter says specifically that your faith can set you free. In Galatians 4:7, Paul writes, "So you are no longer a slave but a child, and if a child then also an heir, through God." Galatians 5:1 reminds us, "For freedom Christ has set us free. Stand firm, therefore, and do not submit again to a yoke of slavery." We catch glimpses of this truth every now and again.

We give away our freedom faster than just about anything else in our lives. People do sacrifice in political and judicial terms, but mostly we let it slip away. Paul speaks of freedom as an inheritance that is one of our most valuable gifts, if we are willing to surrender. We need to quit thinking of surrender as waving a white flag and giving up all hope. It's the opposite. When we don't surrender to love, we lose our freedom as we fight with our fears, anxieties, judgments, and death itself. Surrendering to love is saying "I will let the internal fight cease and not let those things undo me. I will let everything go so I can be free." To be sure, grief and death are formidable opponents that give us reasons to not be free and to fear. You and I are free. We are free from all the bounds that keep us in prison for no reason. We are free to be as bold as we want.

Paul and many other saints claim that surrendering to love binds us to each other. Dietrich Bonhoeffer, who gave up everything and was imprisoned for his faith, says that freedom is not a quality of man. "Anyone investigating man to discover freedom finds nothing of it." Why? Why can we not find that quality in a human being? Bonhoeffer says because "freedom is a relationship between two persons. Being free means 'being free for the other,' because the other has bound me to him. Only in relationship with the other am I free."

Over the years, Magdalene women have recounted the unbelievable insights they had after they had been arrested. Several women have said that you would think their freedom was being taken away. Instead, it was actually the day they were finally set free. They were set free from the prisons of addiction and horrible violence that would have held them until their deaths unless a radical and nonjudgmental love helped change their course. They were set free from the fear of being robbed or raped by people who used them as a commodity. Many people, not just the Magdalene women, are confined to internal and external prisons that keep them suffering without any lock or key. The prisons begin to surround them in their childhoods like chain links built by the terror of child rape and trauma. Shana, one of the graduates and a great ambassador of the program, recently said, "Now I live because I want other women to know freedom." She has bound herself to others still on the streets, preaching so that others may know love.

When we cast off the shackles of judgment, when we

feel the power of the saints, and when we break the chains of oppression for one another, we are on our way to freedom. Freedom is the way we are bound to one another without anxiety, without fear of death, without worrying about judgment. Galatians 5:13–14 tells us, "For you were called to freedom, brothers and sisters; only do not use your freedom as an opportunity for self-indulgence, but through love become slaves to one another. For the whole law is summed up in a single commandment, 'You shall love your neighbor as yourself.'" You are free to move into the deepest axioms of creation, beyond all borders that would enslave you, whatever those might be. You are not male or female in that freedom. You are not black or white in that freedom. You are not old or young in that freedom. You are the embodiment of love, and no one can take that away: not prison, not sickness, not failure, and not death.

As we learn from the past and each other that we are free to live, the next step in gaining insight is to let go of all the things that would hold us down. Tea can be a very simple reminder that we need to let go all the time. I was moving furniture back after a gathering at my house and noticed a glass of old iced tea sitting on the back of the couch where I must have missed it during the cleanup. It wasn't pretty. It was dark and moldy, and without sipping it I felt sure it would taste rotten. That cup is the taste of things we hold on to but have no use for. It is the taste of not drinking the gift we were given but setting it aside and thinking we will get back to it. A cup of tea does not last forever. It is offered to us and we have the freedom to drink it, but we can't hide it away. In the practice of tea ceremonies, there is a saying that "this meeting is but once in a lifetime."[17] When we look into the half-drunk, lukewarm brown liquid in the bottom of the cup, it reminds us of all that we didn't partake of in our lives: friendships, gifts, untouched insight, undiscovered freedom.

I worry that all the planning of a café will turn as stale as the cup of tea and the vision of freedom will be like a cloud that passes us by. As we continue to cut costs and cut corners, the initial dream is becoming a dismal reality. Staring into the unrenovated space at Thistle Farms is like looking into a cup of old, nasty tea, and it's easy to remember how sometimes it feels like things all go to pot.

It is not possible to go back and drink the teas that have gone bad. There is a time to drink the tea and cup we have been given. When its time of sweetness is over, hanging on to it does no good. This tea reminds me that no feeling of elation or discouragement is final; they both pass, and so we move on in faith. Faith is not a feeling; it is the way that surrounds us. It is a good and right thing to be a bit sad and then wash it down the sink. We will brew new golden teas and keep working to raise the money. It's time to brew a new cup of tea and see who is willing to drink from it. Ecclesiastes reminds all those searching for freedom that there is a time and purpose for everything under heaven. There is a time to build this movement and to work to make this dream come true. We have the freedom and insight to make it happen, and we do not need to let it pass us by and then feel bitter.

A group from Thistle Farms has met with a sister group in Atlanta several times about beginning their own community for women coming off the streets. They are a dedicated group, but they haven't yet found a singular vision or the insight to carry it through. This will be the fifth city to launch a sister community for Magdalene and Thistle Farms. We want to enable them to create this new venture and to join in the work of other groups that want to help women coming out of trafficking so they don't have to go to Nashville or New Orleans to find a sanctuary. According to the 2005 FBI status report, Atlanta is one of the top cities in the United States for trafficking women between the ages of eleven and fourteen.

On one particular trip we were invited into the beautiful home of a woman hosting a party to raise money for a house for women who have been trafficked in Atlanta. The interior design contained art and relics from her journeys to Africa, Asia, and Europe. After about an hour of the party, I grew restless and started looking around at her beautiful collections. On a top shelf were two big, square Chinese ceramics. They were very old blue and white porcelain tea boxes, like the ones used to transport tea across the tea routes.

Looking at the chests and remembering their history felt like seeing a statue at the Vatican or admiring a painting at the Guggenheim. To see them is to glimpse into understanding and wisdom. You could imagine the routes tea traders had taken and how the teas were stored. I asked her if I could take them down and look at them. I wanted to touch the tea boxes and get a feel for what it was like on that road from China to Mongolia. Just as it was when I went to an actual tea garden, it felt important to touch with my own hands and see with my own eyes to gain a better understanding of tea's journey. As I felt inside the smooth, cool interior of one box I was reminded about how the image of a journey is always easier than the journey itself.

New understanding can come in the slow study and deliberate work of making dreams come into reality. But sometimes it comes in sweet epiphanies where a window into a new idea or a clearer image of a feeling that has been stirring rises in us. There we were, at a simple party, and as I reached into that old tea box, I could feel that those of us who were gathered at her house were participating in an ancient call for justice. I could imagine that even as the tea was being traded, people were concerned about the well-being of the pickers and were trying to make sure the tea and the people were safe. Just as there is nothing older than trafficking humans, so too are people protesting against trafficking and working toward justice. Touching the tea box offered me an insight into the reality of ancestors who walked with real bodies and real problems just like ours, the pathways where tea and women were traded, and have spoken out for justice and freedom.

We can imagine the rugged ancient roads where the tea boxes were strapped to horses and made their way through thick jungles and mountain passes. The dangers on the road to these beautiful porcelains and the tea they contained would be real and fill the traders with an alert sense of robbers lurking in shadowed trees and thick brush. The people carrying the tea in this stunning old box would be exposed on those roads to the harsh realities that can be poured out in this world. The women we serve are as beautiful and precious as fine porcelain tea boxes. They have been as vulnerable as the tea traders crossing old paths on dangerous roads. What we are doing in helping Atlanta is as old as the boxes before me. This is an old path; we are walking it for the first time, so it feels new to us.

My understanding of tea's history, healing, and gifts has slowly been unfolding. I am grateful for that new understanding and the freedom that comes with it. But I would not be honest if I did not also admit that there are mornings when the tea ritual and the lessons it presents feel boring. They feel like school in midsemester, or a sermon where you know there is so much more to go and you don't want to sit through it. Understanding brings gratitude, humility, and wisdom, but it is hard to stay present always to receive those gifts. My journey into tea had reached the yearlong mark, and no conclusion was in sight. Any of us can grow weary of having to keep learning about a topic that has become too familiar. It is why people put hobbies on back burners, or take a break from church, or quit volunteering. Sometimes the shine just wears off. The tea that once looked like a golden halo can look bland. But when we feel bored pursuing the dream, that is when it is time to keep going. That is the time to not give up. That is when the cloud of witnesses speaks again and tells us to keep going and praying for understanding.

*I am the youngest of eleven children. My mother passed away when I was thirteen. I remember being unable to process this tragedy with my siblings, who were busy with their own lives, or my father, who lived across the street with his new family. Her death was a catalyst to the men who introduced drugs to my life. At sixteen, I was pregnant. By nineteen, I had three children and was selling marijuana for money; and by twenty-six, I had smoked crack for the first time and was hooked. During my addiction, my kids moved in with various family members. I lost my apartment and ended up on the streets. At various times I would try recovery, but nothing worked. My niece, who had gone through the program, put my name on the waiting list for a bed. After years and more stints in jail, a spot finally opened up for me. I began working on my recovery in 2008. I thank God for Becca and for this program. I never thought I would be at this point. I wanted my life back. I promised God by the time I turned forty, I'd be off drugs and have a good husband. I don't have the husband yet, but that's okay because I'll be six years clean in July! To the new women in the program, I can open up and tell them, once you give this place a chance, you realize you are in the right place. I know I couldn't handle this life without putting my spiritual life first.*

—Tasha

Even when we are not inspired we are called by the saints to drink the cup and don't let it go to waste. Even in boredom, understanding is coming and reminding me the money will be there to finish the café. The boredom of the campaign is a side effect of the waiting. As I sip the last drops of this tea, I understand the boredom just means I am gearing up to make the final tasks necessary to finish the campaign for the café. If we get bored, it probably means we are ready for change. I need to get past my bored self and do some work to finish the café.

Elations in the clouds, letting go of old stale ideas, touching the past and feeling bored by the sameness of the work can offer all of us rich ground for new understanding. A library is laid out before us all daily to give us new understanding if we can stay open long enough to learn the lessons. Recognizing the events, ruts, and epiphanies present all around us is a matter of focus that tea can help make clear. The way of tea is to see it all as a gift and then let the experiences go. What we are left with is fortitude and clarity on how we can be headed in the right direction.

# Chapter Ten

# TEA FOR TWO

## Gunpowder Tea

Gunpowder tea sounds like some kind of caffeine-infused energy. It is named for the way the leaves roll up like tiny pellets after being steamed or pan-fired. Unlike other teas, it does not go through the curing process, so it has a more grassy taste. This type of green tea is considered one of the healthiest forms of tea because it has a large amount of the original nutrients. It possesses the most catechins of all teas, containing powerful antioxidants, and it is said to lower cholesterol.

Gunpowder green tea is a joy to watch steep. To make the tea, heat the water to 175 degrees and let the tea float in the water. There are pots designed specifically for gunpowder tea with filters in the spout. Using this type of pot will prevent leaves from floating in your cup, but you can still see the magic of the gunpowder tea, leaves that individually unfurl like small flags. Just add about 2 teaspoons to a pot, add a floral leaf like a jasmine, and watch. It should steep in about 5 minutes.

I WENT FOR A WALK with a piping-hot cup of gunpowder green tea in winter and had to laugh. At one point, I'd thought that we might be a month or so away from opening, but we still hadn't reached our financial goal, the demolition hadn't begun, and we hadn't remodeled the space or carved out four big windows to let the light flood in. As I sipped, I marveled at a big oak tree that looked like a skeleton of a body in an X-ray machine. Will this café be like a skeleton tree, or will it take on buds and leaves and come to life? It's always hard to look at a wood in winter and remember that in the spring it will leaf out and by summer be full of lush green and long grasses. The woods in December feel like a vertical graph, and seem completely dead. It is beautiful because it's easy to see the cardinal's nest and mistletoe. It feels quieter in the winter, as if it is truly laid to rest.

We got a notice today that the engineer cannot give us the go-ahead until we fix some issues in the plans. We can't begin renovations until we get the stamp of approval. So we have to go back and redo the plans and just keep hoping the money will come soon so we can begin. I am aware that the period of waiting has just increased. Like most capital projects in the not-for-profit world where shoestrings hold dreams together, we just put the date out there farther into the future and pray new growth comes. Wondering and waiting for visions to come true is what the season called

Advent is all about. We will watch and wait and dream of leafy green trees full of new life as we appreciate the stillness of skeleton oaks.

Tea helps you dream quietly. Advent should be listed on a list of theologically endangered species in the whirl of a Christmas culture that pulls you in like a carny to a sideshow. Advent is supposed to be four weeks of preparing our hearts, minds, and bodies to receive the incarnate gift of love. When we dream of how love can become flesh and bone, it feels like there is usually a divide between who we are and who we long to be. Between how things are and how we long for them to be. Between the reality of the world and the way we dream of the first garden in Eden.

As I stir a dollop of honey into my deep brown tea, I think the simplest thought, *This is it.* In the sip of gunpowder tea, I felt a spirit rise in me. I was trying to think Advent thoughts about watching and waiting and the need to surrender, but as those thoughts tried to rise with the steam, I could taste Christmas. *Surely it can't be that easy,* came the next thought. Books, lectures, and rituals surround the popular holiday. But the feeling of Christmas rose on a wave of grace. It was a surprise to me that beyond thinking or doing, something from nowhere fills us with new life and reminds us that we are in the presence of love, always.

The beautiful embodiment of love came pouring in over a cup of tea on a bleak midwinter morning. It came like a wave of grace between the endless tides of worry against the shore of my heart. The wave didn't trickle in but washed over the whole scene. It didn't seem possible that I could be surprised by a wave of joy in the midst of brooding about money and delays on the café. In the midst of the tireless Christmas rush glaring as blatantly as the blinking lights festooning houses, everyone should want to brew a cup of tea at Advent. Green tea during this time helps us cross that chasm between the longing and the coming true as a space for hope bridges the two. The moment carried me like evergreen trees that never lose their color. So while the joy was there, joining me, I drank and felt my Christmas gift. The kind of gift you know might be fleeting so you savor it like a rainbow or mist in mountains in the morning. My gift was feeling how time turns liquid in the presence of Christmas. It becomes a fluid concept through which we travel.

Christmas can all at once carry us back two thousand years to the story of the birth of Jesus, then in the next breath we can remember a Christmas from childhood or wonder what the next day will hold. This powerful spirit can break open time and offer it to us like a soothing hot tea. When we drink from the spirit offered to us, we move into the space where the temporal and eternal kiss. We believe things we had spent our days questioning. When we taste the Christmas spirit, we can imagine a peaceable future, a reconciled past, and a present filled with the gift of hope.

Advent isn't the wallflower at a Christmas party. Instead, Advent is the lead dancer that invites us to the dance floor. If we join her, we can feel Christmas come sweeping in on her train and dance with us. We can feel a deep joy in the bottom of even an empty cup that overflows with promise.

There is great joy in knowing that the dichotomy between the urgency to stay busy and the peace that passes understanding can be bridged by a lingering cup of tea. A quiet cup of tea in Advent can calm a storm and spur a weary soul to action.

The gift of Christmas is found within this Advent season, and so love is present and abiding even in the watching and waiting. No other knowledge could bring me such joy. All of us at Thistle Farms will have to honor Advent in spurts and starts and stolen moments with cups of tea washed in love's presence. We can hold the season with a prayer at a stoplight or lingering breaths before we stretch in the morning.

With Advent eyes and hearts, we can see the stars as a heavenly host leading us home and working hard, trusting that Christmas will be there, waiting for the right moment to join in the dance. I put my cup of tea in the sink and offer another Advent prayer that the grants for the café that we have yet to hear about will come. The prayer is similar to the prayers of my childhood, "Oh please, oh please." Prayer is not about its efficacy; it's about unburdening the thought from my head. To fully engage in a season of waiting, we are invited to release the worry and fears using whatever words come. A prayer for patience and hope in Advent is simply a prayer to turn our burdens over like the cup in the sink so there is no residue left at the bottom. We empty the vessel so that new tea can be poured. The ritual of turning a cup over can be a beautiful part of practicing the way of tea. We can imagine letting all the spinning and tiresome thoughts that stick with us like old leaves in the bottom of a cup be washed out.

In a tea ceremony, there are moments where students can ask the tea master questions. The answers usually point to the simplicity and purpose of an empty vessel and a quiet heart. During Advent, may we also be empty vessels, with quiet hearts.

Just as I stilled my heart in celebration of Advent, it was over. It is unbelievable to me how that happens on the spiritual journeys we all take. When we finally let go and settle in, everything changes or the thing we struggled to resolve takes care of itself. Just as we resolved to live in a spirit of Advent and accept the café's unknown time frame, I got a phone call letting me know that Christmas had come early. Just like that. A simple phone call changed the whole season in the building of a dream. The stress of fundraising was over. We were called into the office of the president of Bank of America in Tennessee. After a few moments, he asked us simply, "Who do I give the check to?"

We didn't jump up and down, but we did give a big "wooohoo" at the elevator. It was enough to get going. Now we could move ahead under the leadership of Courtney and the lead volunteer, Kathy Nelson, with a business plan, branding, and interior design. We needed to train six women as baristas, pick a menu, and invite people to partake. Thank God for all the staff and volunteers who have carried this burden together and will continue to take these issues apart piece by piece. They put together something more beautiful than any of us could have imagined. The goal is simply to surrender to the journey and trust that love will carry us to where we need to go, but it's always a complete surprise when love sweeps us up. So in the morning light at the close of the Advent season, a cup of loose-leaf green tea accompanies my pondering of the idea of surrender. I think about all the people throughout the ages who have surrendered to support the longer and much harder Advents than I had just gone through. I thought of the women plucking tea leaves for years in Sri Lanka waiting for better wages. I thought of the men in China waiting to be shipped to India in the nineteenth century who had never left the shores of their own country. I even thought about my own mom, who waited and waited for the scales of justice to tip in favor of widows while she sipped tea and wondered how the family would make it.

## A Beautiful and Humbling Experience

*I am happy. I am hopeful, humbled, and blessed. There was a time when I did not believe these things. My addiction was such a high-risk, violent lifestyle that was a requirement to pretend to be a "bad-ass," and you had better be convincing or you would not survive. It was a cutthroat world I lived in.*

*When I arrived at Thistle Farms, it was a new and unfamiliar world. People were loving and kind. My first thoughts were that everyone lacked sincerity and that it would not last. I could not have been more wrong.*

*For example, last year Becca said, "I want to open a café." I was thinking that would be nice. We had a space but zero money. She put out the word and droves of kind, loving, and generous folks started randomly popping up. I watch the whole community join in the effort.* A most beautiful and humbling experience! *Musicians, artists, teacup donations, demolition teams, fundraisers, painters, and you. I want to thank everyone for their help. If you are reading this, then I would like to thank you for your willingness to step beyond the stereotype that women like us don't recover and ask you to come in to support us.*

—Jennifer, Thistle Stop Café pioneer

It requires surrender to live with an Advent spirit. Advent asked us to believe it is enough to keep working and struggling, and trust that we can surrender our agendas and timelines to love. Surrender is not losing a fight or waving a white flag as all hope is lost. Surrender in love looks more like the internal fight ceasing as trust comes in. We wave a white flag in defeat to love. It's not giving up, it's giving in to. Surrendering to love is saying I will let everything else go so that I am free. Discouragement moves aside and petty issues are seen for the interlopers that they are. In the surrender we can feel an opening toward the people we live and work with daily. We can forgive ourselves for our blindness and quick tongues. The path ahead looks a bit straighter and easier to navigate. We can choose to give up our fear, our control, our complacency, all for love's sake.

In the history of tea, there was no finer time for linking tea to justice than in the Boston Tea Party, right in the midst of Advent in December 1773. It was a time of great surrender for the sake of great ideals. During the night, a group of colonists boarded British ships and threw 342 chests of tea into Boston Harbor. It is hard to imagine the sacrifice they made on many levels. They risked the safety and well-being of their families as well as their own futures. They surrendered to a higher cause and found a great ally in tea. I wonder if any of the men stuffed their pockets with a few containers of loose-leaf tea before toppling the crates into the harbor. They might have thought of it as an act of kindness to their friends and families. They probably had no time as they hurled crates and then ran for their lives, but I hope one or two took some and drank that tea and remembered that night and what ensued.

The Boston Tea Party was an act of political protest about how we should live in community. This act was not a protest over high taxes (the Tea Act being protested actually had lowered the tax on tea) or high prices (the lowered taxes reduced the price of tea below that being charged by smugglers). These colonists were focused on how we tax and take care of our business together. The problem was not that there was a tax on tea but that the tax had been imposed by an external power. "No taxation without representation" is a call for a just community that serves the needs of its own people. "The Destruction of Tea at Boston Harbor," as the event was originally called, was a step in dismantling the British Empire and domination by a foreign power.

That tea party in the middle of the night in Boston has

been a reminder to people to solve problems and fulfill aspirations through compromise, sacrifice, and collaboration. Tea is a symbol that, in the quest to be more equitable, working together in pursuit of shared goals is a gift. Compromise is a respecter of persons; all who come to the table bring truths and values that should be acknowledged and appreciated. The country's greatest triumphs often have come when this inclusive approach has been honored.

The surrender and community inherent in the Boston Tea Party call to mind similar selfless acts found in the Gospels. The disciples' Advent lasted three years as they wended their way toward Jerusalem. All along the way they kept surrendering to empty themselves enough to fill their hearts with love. In the ministry of the disciples in the Gospel story, there are four passages in which Jesus preaches about seeds and nature. Jerusalem was occupied, and the disciples were encountering poverty and oppression, prostitutes and pain wherever they went. Yet to preach about revolution, Jesus describes mustard seeds and fig trees. *The revolutions I am interested in find their roots in this approach.* They look at small acts of great faith, of being unafraid to speak the truth that we can love everyone and be loved because every human being is made in the image of God.

Tea leaves and mustard seeds last longer than most political leaders. They are small but wonderful guides that can lead us to the table of hope that lives beyond political structures and into community that loves the most radically—without judgment. Jesus and his disciples were called people "on the way." They were on their way to walk a three-year journey that they could have covered in three weeks. On the way they kept loving everyone they met, sitting and sharing a cup of some hot beverage, and considering seeds and birds and lilies of the field, until their hearts were ready to lay down for the love of the whole world.

The American revolutionaries surrendered much of their lives, their livelihoods, and their peace when they dumped the tea in the harbor. In surrendering to their cause, they made room for it. They gave up so much to perform this act. They surrendered to liberty and made sacrifices to support their vision of freedom.

Thankfully, our history is full of instances in which individuals and groups have engaged in sacrificial acts, in which they have surrendered things of value for the sake of justice. Mohandas Gandhi modeled a lifetime of such self-deprivation. Humans value few things more than their personal freedom. Yet Gandhi willingly and repeatedly surrendered his freedom for the cause of Indian independence from Great Britain. He was imprisoned several times, from the arrest in 1908 for his first nonviolent refusal to cooperate, through his 1922 arrest for "bringing or attempting to excite disaffection towards His Majesty's Government established by law in British India," until his release from Aga Khan's palace at the age of seventy-five.

A dramatic and pivotal point in the march to Indian independence was Gandhi's 240-mile walk to the sea to produce salt. Even though salt was freely available through the evaporation of seawater, Indians were forced to buy it from the colonial government and pay a new tax. In the tropical climate of India, salt is vital to replace the sodium lost by sweating. Gandhi was not the only one arrested; by the end of the month, sixty thousand Indians were imprisoned by the British in response to the salt protest. For all of these people, and tens of thousands more who risked arrest, the cause of justice overwhelmed any sense of personal liberty. They surrendered their own freedom for the freedom of a nation.

All kinds of justifications and rationalizations keep us cosseted and unwilling to let go. I still hold back so much even as I make the community of Thistle Farms and the priesthood my life's work. I still hold on to exit plans and pay into a retirement account. I wonder how much more love I would experience if I didn't hold back and really surrendered it all. I still pray there is a bridge that crosses the divide between where we are and where we want to be; I recognize that while our hands are full and pockets stuffed, that bridge will be harder to cross. I can see what is written in the bottom of this cup before I take another sip. It's a message that reminds me there is enough spirit to carry us over that bridge on hope.

I still can't believe the waiting is over. All the worries and anxieties are past memories, and the gift has arrived. A person visited Thistle Farms and handed us the beautiful check we were told was coming from the office of Bank of America's president in Tennessee. The thought of a big pile of money in the bank sends me dancing upstairs at work. We did it!—except the part where we have stamped drawings for codes, a building permit, an equipment list written, a staff, logos, and furniture. This will all come. I do believe; I do believe.

Yesterday at Thistle Farms the spirit of Christmas settled into the room. We had outpaced the previous year's Internet sales and raised enough money to open the new café so we can welcome six new employees. We gathered together as a community. Women without prompting or rehearsal recalled Christmases past spent on the streets looking for money and eating fast food burgers in hotel rooms rented by the hour. Women remembered childhoods of visiting their moms in prison or grieved having no memories of Christmas at all. They wept as they remembered relatives and friends they had lost or who were sick this Christmas. Then a woman talked about celebrating the birth of Jesus for the first time in her life. The conversation moved freely into comments about this Christmas and the joy of being in community. In that circle, we traveled through Christmas seasons with each other, not boxed by time but moving through memory and hope. It didn't matter how many Christmases were gone or what future Christmases held. All that mattered was that in this Christmas, we felt healed. We had surrendered enough in Advent to receive the gift of Christmas.

*Chapter Eleven*

# TEA RESOLUTIONS

## Chai Tea

Chai tea comes from the Indian subcontinent where *"chai"* is simply the generic term for "tea" in Hindi. Chai is black tea brewed with selected spices and milk. My friend Susan and I made this delicious tea in her cabin on a cold January morning and vowed we would try to make it every day. Consider increasing or decreasing the amount of cinnamon and cardamom depending on your taste.

　1½ cups water
　¾-inch stick cinnamon
　7 cardamom pods
　7 whole cloves
　⅔ cup milk
　6 teaspoons sugar
　3 teaspoons unperfumed loose black tea

Put water into a saucepan. Add cinnamon, cardamom, and cloves. Bring to a boil. Cover, turn heat to low, and simmer for 10 minutes. Add milk and sugar. Bring to a simmer again. Add tea leaves, then cover and turn off the heat. Strain tea into 2 cups and serve immediately.

TEA CAN BE A simple means by which we all can make new resolutions. In the few minutes it takes to steep a proper cup of tea, we can rediscover how easily and beautifully everything can be transformed. Water, the simplest form of liquid designed to hydrate us, takes on a complicated fullness of life. The water turns dark as the aroma from the wilting leaves awakens the spirit. The hot elixir isn't meant to be chugged. Its steamy perfection calls and awakens our gentleness and patience. It asks us to believe in the possibility that as we consume a thousand cups, we may be transformed like the water before us. The steamy beverage invites a moment of silence to consider the beauty of change and wonder. The time for steeping is time offered to us to think about where we are, where we would like to be, and how we might possibly make it. I have used the time waiting for the water to boil or for the water to turn a golden brown imagining how I could lose weight, get on a plane to Africa, or turn into a good cook and make something wonderful for my family.

As I drank a homemade chai on a freezing morning, I welcomed my New Year thoughts. In the twenty minutes it took me to make this cup, I thought about the hospice in Gaborone, Botswana, where my family and I traveled to serve people living with HIV/AIDS. One morning we arrived at nine thirty and there were about nine people in respite care sitting under a porch in the bright Kalahari sun. They had been talking about treatments and health issues, but as we sat down, the social worker said to the group, "It's tea time."

Just like that, all the conversation about what medicines and treatments they needed to keep them alive was laid aside as tea was set out for everyone. Social workers and nurses on the front lines of the global AIDS crisis stopped midmorning to take tea. It was a lesson in how to achieve peace in the fight for justice. I drank that tea with a new resolve to live like this: fighting for justice and living in peace. The teatime that morning helped me see the differences in the blue shades of a sky and notice the nest suddenly visible in the tree we had walked by many times on our visits to the hospice. This tonic is a medicine that can start the morning for tea drinkers', thankful for life itself and wondering how to live more deeply in all the moments we have been given. That is how tea can transform us and can be at the heart of resolutions.

The tradition of making New Year's resolutions is more than four thousand years old.[18] Year-end is a perfect time to reflect back and set goals for the future. I haven't set very many New Year's resolutions apart from my continual resolution to lose five pounds and exercise more. We resolve to make amends or change, not just on January 1 or on Ash Wednesday but when we feel like we need to do something different. Resolutions are decisions either to do something or to refrain from doing something. Resolutions seem like a natural way to try to live a better life. Making resolutions is easy-peasy. The problem is in keeping them.

## Pu-erh Tea

Thistle Farms spent $120 on a single cake of pu-erh tea from a Chinese tea shop on the West Coast. I made this lavish purchase as a gift for the employees. The pu-erh was buried for seven years and then wrapped in beautiful thin tissue paper stamped for authenticity. I brought it home and announced a tea party for the eight women in the company who will help launch the café. Before I served the pu-erh, I poured a sweet oolong into small cups. The women tasted it and discussed whether they liked it or not. The invitation I offered after this first tasting and before I passed the cake of pu-erh around was to breathe in the gift of tea and to taste what it could offer. Don't think about coating the gift with sugar or softening the sensation. Don't think so much whether you like it or don't like it. Think about understanding how and why it tastes like it does.

As each woman breathed the round, flat cake of pu-erh in and then tasted a freshly poured cup, the first effect of this rich tea enlivened the spirit of the group. "It tastes like a country road," said a woman from the Midwest. "It tastes like the earth," one woman said after turning up her nose at first. Her family had owned a farm. Then a young woman new to the program said almost as a throwaway line, "It tastes like my grandmother." Her grandmother might

*(Continued)*

have been the closest person to the earth she had ever known, and her memory rose in the flavor and aroma. A good earthy tea can raise the memory of love close to earth and near the heart.

Over the past twenty years I've discovered the importance of community in keeping resolutions. One small example is that in my own resolve to practice yoga, I've learned that it helps to have a friend to sign up with, a class to go to, and children who are patient when dinner is late. Anyone seeking to make a change or walking the road of recovery knows the importance of community to hold them up and hold them accountable. We need each other because the role the community plays in the nature and implementation of resolutions is huge.

But beyond community helping foster individual resolutions, we need to affirm communal resolutions. These help hold the community accountable and keep us on the same path. As the community thrives, our individual lives thrive. Common resolutions foster the common good, which affects us all. One communal resolution is to live out our faith together. We promise to be there for one another in good and bad times, and we promise we'll hold each other up and hold each other accountable. When we are together, the sum is greater than its parts. Common resolutions should be at the heart of our resolutions since they are the key to living in gratitude with meaning in our lives. At Thistle Farms, these communal resolutions are formed purposefully and organically. Every week we read together one of the twenty-four spiritual principles we are trying to live by, and all of us vow to help each other follow those practices. We take a resolution to never shut the door on any one individual, and so we all work toward a plan for helping a woman come home, even if she has relapsed on prostituting or drugs.

Our community gathers twice a year to make our communal resolutions. We sit for a whole day and think through what we can do better and how we can move together to grow the company. This is not strategic planning; it is a recommitment to work together to resolve all the forces that would tear apart the women who work there if they were alone. Living in visions of hospitality almost two thousand years old is at the heart of our resolve to open a café. This café will be a perfect example of living in our Christian ideals of allowing individuals to live in their resolutions.

Recently a new resident came empty-handed to Magdalene directly from an out-of-state prison. She came in with a head full of resolutions and the means to carry out none. She resolved to live a life of recovery, regain custody of her children, restore her health, further her education, and get a job. The gap between her ability and her desires looked as wide as the Grand Canyon. But she came into a community with common goals and purpose that could help her make some headway. The way it began to unfold was remarkable. She told me that when she arrived, her new roommate gave her clothes, shampoo, new underwear, and towels. She said she had never been treated with such kindness. I was tempted to say "Your roommate had received all of those things from others, and so she just gave you what was given to her." But as soon as the thought popped into my head, I knew that is just what we all do. We think we give to others what was ours in the first place, when truly it was given to us and we just share it. Whether it's a towel, a prayer, or a common resolution, we are called to love the world, so we all have to keep changing to love it better. We need a community of faith with a common resolve that believes love will help us live out our dearest resolutions for the sake of the world.

Opening the café is our top communal resolution, and it draws our community closer together. Even though a hammer has not yet hit a nail, you can feel the strength in the community to see this through. It keeps us all moving forward. As much as we don't want to give up on our personal resolutions, we also don't want to let down all the folks who are pouring their hearts into the project. This resolution is calling a community to live and act out their faith in ways that would never be possible alone. The resolution to create the café has a chance at coming to fruition because it is a communal effort. When I imagined the space a year ago, I thought it was a simple idea just to serve tea. After all, people have been serving tea in teahouses for a thousand years. There are countless beautiful stories about teahouses opening in old spaces. No one wrote about being bogged down in permits and the size of the drainage filter in the back room. It is hard to bring resolutions to life. Having community working together makes possible what might be impossible alone.

One of my favorite stories about tea and resolutions comes from the novel *The Paris Wife* by Paula McLain. It describes the early years of Ernest Hemingway in Paris. Hemingway resolved to try to write just one true sentence a day and he ordered his life around that desire. He moved to France, rented an office that was the size of a closet, and made himself sit for hours at his typewriter and write a sentence that reflected the truth of his heart. When he got too cold to work, he would walk to a café and have a cup of tea.

The other important part of resolutions is to make a small step and see how far it carries you. Resolutions are not magical thoughts that happen to us. Resolutions involve a willingness to do the work to make the change possible. For us the first step in this new year was, come hell or high water, to start demolition. Almost always for people to begin a resolution, we have to clear space in ourselves and in this world to bring new life to bear. So, early on a Saturday morning, a group came and picked up sledgehammers and took down walls that needed to go. The dust was so thick in the room we couldn't take pictures or even talk to each other. The thick drywall dust fog was a sign of how it's hard to see, in the first steps of living our resolutions, where we are heading. But the first step is surely a promise that we may get there. The six women—Arleatha, Christy, Jennifer, Terry, Anika, and Ronza—who will start training as baristas and tea servers have been hired and are now on board at Thistle Farms. These pioneers of the café will serve tea and love to a whole community. They represent the reality

163

of the dream. Collectively they are the embodiment of how an idea can change a life. Individually they are a testament to how we can never forget the healing power of love in our lives. We had imagined raising money building a beautiful café; now here is the band of noble women comprising the first team. None has ever worked at a tea shop. They've spent more than twenty-five years in jail and prison combined. More than sixty years if you add in their time on the streets. They've been sexually abused and addicted, but they demonstrate outrageous courage as they venture together on an expedition to an unknown land. All the brokenness the women have known somehow has not thwarted their ability to trust. They are throwing themselves into barista training. They'll learn to serve tea and run a café. It will be a long and glorious journey, I am sure.

One of the women doing the training says she lived under a tree before she came into the community. One day she ran after a car down the middle of the road because she recognized the person driving. It was Regina, one of the first graduates of Magdalene who directs our outreach efforts. The woman flagged Regina down, joined our community, and says she never looked back. When I see her, I see a woman of great strength who made a resolution. She is an inspiration as she takes care of her children and grandchildren after decades on the streets. Her story reminds us we are all capable of making resolutions that can dramatically change our lives and the lives of all those we touch.

Just as we had a plan and were moving forward, I was completely thrown off course. That can happen with resolutions. I was sipping a lemon ginger tea on the porch on a Saturday evening, thinking about what to preach the next morning, when I received a call from my brother-in-law. The wave of grief following the news that my sister, Katie Stevens Garrett, had died, crashed over me.

The universal reaction to that first wave of grief takes us under. It's like moving from quietly walking by a creek and admiring the water to suddenly being completely lost at sea in deep and unknown waters. It comes in a low and sometimes silent wail that we carry within us whether we know it or not. You can see it on a face like a shroud and you can feel it in the air as if it's electric. It's the first signal that you are adrift in an ocean of pain. The hope is to cling to other survivors, keep an eye on the distant shore, and try to trust you will find your way back to solid ground.

Katie died from an aortic aneurism. Until that day, she had been a healthy, happy fifty-six-year-old woman. She was just getting to know her sweet new grandbaby twins. With only one child at home, she was beginning to feel the freedom that comes from being an empty nester. The family gathered at my home to plan her funeral, say good-bye to her body, and figure out what this meant for her kids and husband, who has been disabled for over ten years. Forty members of our family, including my two other sisters and brother, sat around my living room to piece together the whole story, not just of the death but of her life. The teapot whistled on the stove as stories rose from the pictures scattered across the table. We could hear her voice and feel her love, which could never be doused by death, no matter how quickly her death had swept in on us. When I gave Katie's eulogy, it felt like a small way to honor her and help keep her deepest resolutions alive. I said:

Katie was born on Independence Day and took that birthday to heart as she grew up with a beautifully independent spirit that always rooted for the underdog. She was a clear and willing debater for the causes of civil rights and equality. Fiercely competitive in board games and cards, she taught her four younger siblings early on that if she looked at your cards, it's not cheating; it is your fault you didn't hold the cards close to your chest. She was precise about language, another sign of her intelligence and wit. She was invited to join Mensa, didn't have to go to the movies since she could read a book in about the same time, and she loved sciences. Her crowning achievement in her life was easily the gift of her three beautiful and smart daughters. She was a senior chemist that appreciated the precision of a lab and environmental issues. She was beautiful and didn't have a vain bone in her whole body. She would give you the shirt off her back without a thought.

She helped Thistle Farms filter the water for the products, secured a donation from her lab of a dozen tables, and taught us how to calibrate our still to make essential oils. Watching her work in front of the machine all day was an insight into how changing things incrementally makes a big change in the quality of the oils. She reminded me that God was in the details. The image of my sister, the scientist, standing before that machine, a tool of healing and justice, is a symbol that when we do small things, big dreams can come true. She helped us distill all kinds of herbs so that we could make healing oils for people all over the country. She believed that when you distill it all down, we are blessed in our joys and sorrows and riches and in our poverty.

Death doesn't take away our resolve, even if we find ourselves adrift in a sea of grief that washes us in unexpected tears in random parking lots or with a cup of chamomile clutched to our chest. It can renew our desire to live in our resolutions as we make our way back to the safety of the shores. When people we love die, it reminds us that how we live is so important. When we grieve, we see pretty clearly from the vantage point of a wide-open sea that what we do now lives beyond us in our death.

Katie's untimely death leaves me with more resolve to live in the ideals of love all the days of my life. Resolutions are a gift to us and to all those we love who will live beyond us. The saints inspire and give us the courage to live in our best resolutions. How we live will be how we die. If we live in love, we will die in love. So in this season of resolutions, I toast alone in the bleak midwinter to live better, in gratitude, in the days I am given. To resolve to tell the next generation about the loving way the people who came before them tried to live their lives. May all those we grieve be our inspiration to live deep in the truth that love can change the world and heal broken hearts.

*Chapter Twelve*

# TEA RETREATS

## Slow Tea

On retreats, bring everything needed to make slow tea. It's as important as a journal or good book. If you don't prepare what you need to make tea ahead of time, you will be stuck with stale tea bags that have been sitting by the coffeepot for a couple of years. The people who run the retreat will tell you it's because no one drinks tea. My feeling is that if we offered tea as it was intended, everyone would drink it.

**Tea for Retreats**

Take a small tea strainer and a nonbreakable metal thermos. Pack teas that carry the following purpose and great flavor:

**Two floral or lotus teas** that take about 20 minutes to unfold. These are perfect for meditation times as they unfold in the same amount of time people usually sit for a meditation.

**Chai** that has a bit of spice to bring you into awareness and appreciation for the whole wonder of creation.

**Herbal teas** with lavender or chamomile to carry with you for peace.

**A nice green tea** to use daily as a ritual for opening your mind to new thoughts.

WHEN YOU RETREAT EITHER to the mountains in Tennessee or some exotic place, tea is a quiet companion. The thin, dried leaves speak of a patience that waits for the time when we are ready to pour the water and drink. Retreat and tea are like peanut butter and jelly or, better yet, like word and deed. You can imagine the rising of a new thought as you take a sip of tea in front of a fire or in a sacred quiet space. James Norwood Pratt, a notable tea professional, wrote this about tea: "an elixir of sobriety and wakeful tranquility, tea was also a means of spiritual refreshment and the ritual of preparing and partaking of it was an occasion for spiritual conviviality, a way to go beyond this world and enter a realm apart."[19] Taking tea to retreat has been a practice since the tea masters perfected the tea ceremony to be a path of enlightenment and a way of being in itself.

Going on retreat is not pulling away from the good fight; it's a brave act to step back and assess where we are and gather strength for the journey ahead. Retreat is the period our souls long for, to look to the mountains for our strength and wait like the bridegroom for his bride. This is respite, the place we see visions and the wilderness where we wrestle with ourselves. I love the image in the Gospels of the disciples going to a lonely place to find time to focus and talk with their teacher alone. They had to get away from the crowds, not because they didn't love them but so they could love them more.

I packed up bags of thistle seed, cardamom, wild ginger, cinnamon sticks, black and green tea leaves, some lotus tea blossoms, ginger, and lavender, and headed out. One of the scary parts of retreating is that everything keeps going on without you. It's humbling and freeing in the same breath. Construction had begun on the café, and the women had even started training. We can step aside for retreat and the world doesn't miss a second in its orbit. Just when we think we are indispensable, we are reminded that we are not. But while retreats are humbling in that way, they also honor those duties and tasks, as they give us a chance to renew our strength and energy to do our work better.

I need to go away to the mountains for a few days, regain my grounding, and come back with a renewed sense of energy. This retreat is like peeling back enough layers of busyness to get to the heart of the matter, and tea will help take those layers off with grace. Since the days when Lu Yu and the other tea fathers first recognized that tea was a spiritual companion to bring calm and awareness to the heart, tea has been carried by monks and religious guides. Tea can be a consciousness-altering agent that brings us back to our center. It can help settle us long enough to be stirred into the awareness that is necessary in retreat.

I was going on this retreat because it felt like it would be a safe place to cry with my creator. I took my grieving heart on retreat and finally had the time to remember all the details of my sister that I was afraid would slip away.

I remembered all the times she drove us to the mall when our mom was working. How she could blow smoke rings inside other smoke rings, how she did crosswords in pen, and how she loved family. Time slowed down enough for me to take her death in and honor her with memory. People can retreat to focus on resolutions, gain the necessary insight to see a vision through, or simply to rest and feel the power of silence.

Getting there and coming back are bookends that make being on retreat difficult to undertake. Letting our schedules go and removing ourselves is hard to do. Coming back from a period of deep contemplation and stepping back into our lives is even more difficult. We want to hold on to the vision of the mountains and not get bogged down like we were just days before. When I left the cabin sated by tears and tea, I didn't want to jump back into work. Instead of getting back into the swing of things, what I wanted to do was stay in the mountains with the memories of my sister. I could stay another few days and stretch out on the cabin couch with a comforter tucked in close and watch the flames in the fireplace dance. The longing to stay made me feel like I was sitting by James and John and Peter, the disciples, when they asked Jesus to let them stay in the mountains after the transfiguration. They wanted to build a shrine away from the outside world and live with the beauty of dazzling heavenly light. That feeling of wanting to stay on the mountaintop is not hard for us to grasp. This world is hard. We want to stay in that place where we may get a glimpse of Elijah and Moses and the people we love who have died. We want to stay in the safety and beauty of a mountain. Maybe get a glimpse of the back of God's head, like Moses on Sinai. I'll take that. There is this sense that if you are in the mountains, you are apart from this world— that it can't affect you. That you are going to be safe there.

Retreats, though, should remind us that we can be the same person on the mountaintop as we are in the valley of work. We are the same person in the lofty cathedrals of inspiration as we are when we are plodding through the dark corners of our doubts. We only have one life. When Jesus talks about heaven and divine things in the kingdom of God, He doesn't talk about veiled truths that we can never understand. He talks about earthly, simple things like a treasure in a field, a pearl of great value, sowing seeds, or taking dirt and spit and loving someone enough to put it on their eyes to heal them. These earthly images give us a glimpse of heaven. Retreats are not places to reinvent ourselves or pretend we are holier than we actually are. They are places to recollect ourselves so that we can live and not get weary from all the work there is to do.

The story of the transfiguration reminds us that before, during, and after their retreat, the disciples were the same; they just became more themselves. Part of the point of that story is to remind us that heaven is no more in the mountains than it is in the valleys. Retreats can be the bridge between having our heads in the clouds and our feet on the ground walking toward justice. We can be inspired on the mountain, but all inspiration fades without action, no matter how vivid the dream.

The call to retreat is in part a call to remember and to return. The most inspired retreats will fade unless we go back into our lives and live out the call to love right here, with each other. Our actions are love made manifest. Retreats make a piece of heaven feel like a reality on this earth and make this earth a little closer to heaven. We are reminded during the mountaintop experience what a gift all of life is. And everything we do with our stewardship, time, and talents shows our gratitude for that gift. I am so grateful that God doesn't leave us on that mountain no matter how badly we want to stay. Can you imagine when Peter, James, and John whispered in Jesus' ear: *Let's stay in this beautiful place; the authorities will never find us up here. Let's stay where we have visions of those we love who have died. We don't have to leave; we don't have to walk toward our death.* Jesus reminds them that's not what love is about. It's not where we are headed. If we get off the mountain, maybe we can help our communities look a little bit more like heaven.

Sometimes the places of retreat can catch us by surprise. Around this same time, I preached at Grace Cathedral in San Francisco. I arrived early to get a sense of the place; walking in felt like entering Oz. The vaulted ceiling, mural walls, priceless artwork, and stained glass illuminated by hallowed light felt like refuge. I noticed a beautiful sculpture of a mother and child with small candles underneath that could be lit for a donation. As I read the plaque under the statue and how it was given in memory of a beautiful mother, I remembered that we also retreat to heal. We go to heal ourselves so we are able to be the light we are called to be in this world. I felt healed simply by being in that cathedral. I just sat in quiet prayer and awe and let myself heal a bit in the small enclave with an image of the Madonna and child.

This surprise mini-retreat continued as I met the dean of one of the most beautiful cathedrals in North America. Dr. Jane Shaw hails from England and was a professor at Oxford in history for sixteen years prior to coming to the cathedral. The first thing she did was buy me a cup of tea and tell me a few stories about the teahouses in Oxford. I loved that she knew tea, that she knew how to use it as a sign of hospitality and safety, and that she was as grounded as she was intelligent and funny. We became fast friends as she lifted me out of my sadness with Earl Grey and a lilting accent. A good sign that you are in retreat mode is when conversations drift and there is no urgency to get back on task. Retreat language is open-ended and nonjudgmental. It is language that contains hope. The surprise morning retreat carried me from an anxious state through a moment of grief, a touch of healing, respite, and hospitality in the form of tea, to an altar that offers us a place to commune with the eternal.

Our mornings could become mini-retreats if we approached them with sincere hearts and knowledge of our need for healing. While most of us would love to be able to go to the mountains in Jackson Hole or the sacred shrines of Europe or follow holy roads in Spain, sometimes we make retreat wherever we are and with whatever tools we have. That kind of surprise retreat reminds us that we don't always get to choose when we retreat or grieve. Sometimes grief grabs us as we try to hold pain close to our chests. It waits and meets us around a lonely corner and takes us down. Grief can weary any body as it curls up next to us at night and visits our dreams with strange twists that pull us back to childhood. And so we need morning retreats that give us a break even in the midst of busy days. As I am trying to walk this path of professional fundraiser, entrepreneur, and priest alongside grieving sister, my mantra has been walk slow, be gentle, and when you get a chance, head to the hills.

After that morning in the cathedral, I found another surprise retreat on the edge of the San Francisco Bay. As I stood near a pier in the fog, gazing over the water, I thought about how far water will carry us if we are willing to travel out to sea. We are heading from the mountains to the sea and someday will make our way to an ocean that will carry us back to God. Ultimately, retreat is remembering that truth. I sipped tea and sat at the pier with the steam rising from my cup merging into the thick fog, and believed for the first time in weeks that my sister was well. Retreating on a wing and a prayer to our hearts is one of the greatest spiritual gifts we can access. Cultivating that gift has been a practice for centuries in the spiritual life. Take a cup, go on retreat, and carry that peace back into the crazy world. That peace is older than the tea you are sipping and any problems you are facing. Retreating is the gift we have been given to move ahead.

*Chapter Thirteen*

# POURING OUT

## A Recipe for Forage Tea

Sometimes when you are traveling in the woods and hillsides, it's fun to think about what herbs and spices you can forage for that might make a great tea. It's also a great experience just to go into a local market and ask for *té*. On an annual pilgrimage thirty of us make to the Los Ríos area of Ecuador, four women, including myself and my best friend Tara, went foraging. We collected chamomile blossoms and ginger root from the market and then picked lemongrass we had planted two years before. You can gather all of these items in the United States. We also picked up some green tea and a few small limes.

We boiled water in a big pot and steeped the roots and herbs for about ten minutes. The exact amount is still unclear to me because we just added what we had. The next step was to add three green tea bags we had packed with us and let the whole mixture steep for another three to five minutes. Then we poured it all through a strainer into another old pot we found. It was delicious. What made the beverage even sweeter was sharing the pot with the four local women who have been cooking for the group for the past two days. This silly foraged tea was enough to make them stop, sit, and sip the brew with us. We laughed and watched as one of the women finished nursing her baby and spooned a bit of tea into the child's mouth. We sat for about fifteen minutes learning names and sharing recipes. Foraging tea will gather a group and settle a body in travel stress.

THE WORK JUST DOESN'T end; you make tea, drink tea, and before you know it, you are thirsty again. That is what life feels like sometimes: a never-ending thirst that is part of the human condition. It is a thirst for something still a bit out of our reach and something that will fill an emptiness that lingers somewhere between our heads and our hearts. It is a thirst to feel success and wealth on a scale measured by others. It is in this longing that tea really shines. Tea was meant to be poured out, created to soothe the weary spirit, and brewed to satiate our hunger for meaning. Somewhere along even our best journeys of hope there are days we want to call it quits and tune out. Those are the days to make new resolutions, take mini-tea retreats, and then go ahead and pour out our hearts again for love's sake.

Such a day came to me while in a meeting with the head of a foundation who came to visit the café site. Since construction has been delayed due to codes and unforeseen issues, costs have increased, and we have had to go out and find donors to cover salaries for the people hired and waiting for us to open. In the meeting, the man said some nice things about the work but then said that his foundation is concerned that Thistle Farms is trying to do too much instead of focusing on what we already do. He said to me, "Less may be more in this circumstance." I had just finished showing him where the construction was in full swing and served him a steaming cup of rich black tea. I defended our actions quickly and explained that the café was the continuation of the vision of serving. His criticism was too late, but truth be told, it hurt when he said that his "circle of peers" had discussed the café and me. It meant there were folks who thought we shouldn't or couldn't pull it off. He explained he just wanted to let me know the concerns "out there" so I wouldn't be blindsided.

Maybe he is right that we are trying to be too big or do too much. Maybe we're just searching for the next thing that will sate our thirst for success. Maybe we are overstating our ability to serve justice tea and our contribution to a national movement. But maybe he is wrong. Perhaps, in order to sustain a social enterprise, you have to continue to grow. I believe that opening a café is exactly the right thing since we are not only creating products but place. I believe the café can help launch the movement for women's freedom into full gear with Shared Trade and through offering hospitality to the strangers who will come from all over the world to taste hope.

But whether he was right or wrong, what was striking to me was that as he sat there and offered me words to contemplate, he forgot the biggest view of the picture. It's not whether we can be sustained or not, but how it is impossible to sustain a community without taking care of the women who have been broken by people who can look at numbers and fail to see the real bottom line. The real bottom line to me is that no community is well that thinks prostitution is a victimless crime or that we bear no responsibility as a nation in bringing the women safely home. But he kept talking about the need for us to be sustainable, as if he did not bear some part in that equation. I hope someday to invite him into the café, sit down with a proper pot of tea, and offer him one of the sweetest cups of healing tea he has ever tasted. Maybe he will see the great gift he offered the women in the form of the grant and how much better this world is because the women are healing.

The feeling that came over me as he left was not anger but a desire to pour more of my heart into the café. I want to pour tea out as a symbol of how we can love well, even if someone does not accept it. I want to pour tea out not just for this executive, but for all the occasions and for all the people to whom I have said hurtful things. Just the idea that tea is poured out of a pot is enough to contemplate over a cup. Tea is poured out, not meted out in small helpings, as is the case with other foods or even people. It is a Christian notion that an offering is poured out for the sake of the well-being of another. Tea becomes a symbol of the nature of sacrificial love. In the Gospels, Jesus said His blood was "poured out" for the sake of forgiveness. We were created to be poured out. What if every time we poured a pot of tea for a stranger or friend, we were forgiving ourselves and others as freely as the leaves release their healing gifts? Imagine if we could see our heart being poured out with the tea. This could make the world a better place. An idea has been brewing for months that Thistle Farms can host "flash tea parties": unexpected tea events where we pour out tea for strangers and invite them to sit and feel the hospitality and peace tea can offer.

Being poured out for others is a quintessential image of giving in the Gospels. Before Jesus enters Jerusalem, He stops to visit Lazarus, Mary, and Martha. As they're gathered along with guests, Mary takes out an expensive bottle of nard worth the equivalent of $6,000 in today's economy. Mary pours the costly fragrance over Jesus' feet and wipes them with her hair. The liquid must have spilled out onto the floor. The act seems outlandish until we realize that she is preparing Him for burial; then it becomes an act of overwhelming gratitude and love. It feels like one of the most intimate and loving acts in all the Gospels. I imagine she wept as she poured the oil. She had to be pouring out her heart and laying all the hope and brokenness of her life at His feet.

One of the disciples criticizes Mary. The money could have been spent on the poor. This is a hollow response to a generous act. They will still be able to offer charity to people who are poor and work for justice in the name of love. The moral issue is not offering a lavish gift to the people we love. The whole Gospel is rooted in the belief that the moral issue is our reaction to the suffering before us. The truth that Jesus and His disciples were devoted to the healing and serving of others was never in question. This lavish act of love by Mary teaches us how to serve. Her willingness to pour out a huge gift with humility and respect reminds us of our posture while pouring out our lives for the sake of others. Jesus ends the discussion by saying the poor will always be with us. That is a blessing, not a curse. There will always be Magdalene women with us. They will always find their way from the streets of hell to a sanctuary of love as long as we are able to keep such sanctuaries open. Every one of the women will be a blessing.

Mary's pouring out of the oil onto the feet of Jesus leads us to a hallowed group. The story is a reminder to give extravagantly and lavish love on those we love but who won't be with us forever. Mary was painfully aware that Jesus was heading toward Jerusalem and into the heart of the occupied nation to confront authority. She gave Him the best of what she had. Like Mary, we must learn to pour out our fine oils and our finest teas. With the dedication of a religious act, I have tried to pour out tea daily for my husband. Serving and pouring the tea are an act of great gratitude for me that he has walked with me this whole way without asking much of me in return. I pour his tea with a full heart and without any need for him to reciprocate this act. I carry the tea to our room early in the morning so he gets to drink it before he has to wake up to the all the demands that the day will bring. Pouring tea out for him feels different to me from just serving tea to a group. This is more humbling and intimate. It is a glimpse of what it means to love in a way that you could lay your life down for another without the person even asking.

There are so many ways that I don't allow myself to be poured out. Ego creeps in and ruins perfectly good and humble tea that was willing to be steeped and poured for a friend. Those are the days I think I have just enough tea for myself or worry that the world may have short-served me or overcharged me for tea. Sometimes I think there is no reason to pour it out, because then I will have less. I don't want to pour it for someone who has neither the inclination nor the education to appreciate the quality of tea offered. Sometimes I recollect the person has never given me a cup of tea. Other days I feel like my cup is not close to half full due to no fault of my own. It just feels like there is barely enough for me to get through the day. But truly those are the days we most need to pour out a whole pot of tea and offer it to someone with an open and grateful heart. It is on those days we learn the lessons of abundance: that love is poured out for us all and that all the tea in China doesn't begin to match the quantity or quality of the mercy and love we have been given. When we empty ourselves, we are filled by a grace we didn't know could rise in us. That is how we learn that whatever pots of tea we can pour for others are simply tokens of gratitude. Tea poured out is an offering of our hearts in gratitude for life. And so in the amount of time it takes to pour out a simple pot of tea, it is possible to reposition our hearts.

Tea poured out is poetry in action. And poetry becomes a state of being where the private longings of our hearts become loud enough for us to hear. To pour tea out is a sign that we want to experience this world like the poets themselves. Thoughts that begin as stirrings in our hearts barely above a soft whisper begin to simmer in a teapot. Once poured out and taken in, they become strong thoughts that ring in our ears like a loud wind. All the poetry and all the deep thoughts are right there, right there in the leaves steeping. The poetry of tea is there for our taking, but we have to be willing to stop and take a seat. We have to be willing to take the time to heat the water. We have to be open to a thought stirring as gently as a bit of honey melting in the bottom of a teacup.

## The Perfect Cup of Tea Recipe

First, use Indian or Ceylonese tea. Second, use a teapot of china or earthenware. Third, warm the pot beforehand by placing it on the stove. Fourth, make the tea strong. Fifth, put the tea straight into the pot. Sixth, take the teapot to the kettle as the water should be boiling at the moment of impact. Seventh, give the pot a good shake before allowing the leaves to settle. Eighth, use a cylindrical mug. Ninth, pour the cream off the milk before using it for the tea. Tenth, pour the tea into the cup first. "This," wrote George Orwell, "is one of the most controversial points of all; indeed in every family in Britain there are probably two schools of thought on the subject. The milk-first school can bring forward some fairly strong arguments, but I maintain that my own argument is unanswerable. This is that, by putting the tea in first and stirring as one pours, one can exactly regulate the amount of milk whereas one is liable to put in too much milk if one does it the other way around." Finally, eleventh, drink the tea without sugar.[20]

It is in the act of pouring out tea like our love into this world that we can travel on a tea leaf and a prayer to poetry, centeredness, compassion, or whatever spiritual gift that needs watering. Tea poured out for others and ourselves is the outward and visible sign that we are tending to our interior life as well as serving our neighbors as ourselves. Pouring tea for ourselves is a ticket to travel with private visions and even fantasies that are not bound by time and space. We do not travel linearly, but where our spirit leads us. We may take flight and sip tea in Narnia with C. S. Lewis, drink with Mohandas Gandhi on the eve of independence, or even sip with Ernest Shackleton in the Weddell Sea at the South Pole. And we may just sit and daydream in the space we don't put words to for others to read. Tea will travel with us to all those places, not just as a willing partner but as a wise guide. It is tea that allows those spaces and thoughts to move in us.

Tea is being poured out everywhere, even on the floor as a stain at Thistle Farms. The women are getting trained to pour chai tea lattes with heart-shaped foam. The new drywall is being installed, and the 150-year-old red pine floor from the tobacco barn of the warehouse of Al Gore Sr. is stacked and ready to be laid by a crew of a hundred volunteers. We have kept going even though there are still issues with codes and worries about money. "The more momentum we can build, the harder it will be to stop it" is the new theory. Once we pour our hearts and resources into this project, it will be impossible to get them back into the teapot!

This floor, carried and laid by volunteers, reminds me of the great pouring out of charity. The floor is made to be laid with tongue and groove, meaning each piece has a long rim on one side that must be sanded to fit perfectly into the groove on the next piece. It is time consuming and truly a labor of love. The contractor said he is not a fan of reclaimed wood, mostly because of the huge investment of time and patience required to lay it. In some ways using this floor is not the most economical approach. But it is a way for a hundred people who want to be a part of this unfolding story of hope to participate. We are going to put a coffee-and-tea stain on the wood to help bring it back to its old self after we lay and sand it. Volunteers pour their hearts into this floor, then for years will bring their friends and family into this space and see what they helped build. The logo came back from the volunteer designer and is simply a circle of tea leaves with "Thistle Stop Café" written in the middle. I do believe it's just about perfect for us.

A wonderful landscape architect, Tara Armistead has designed an outdoor garden with trees to surround a deck, which is made from huge planters. This truly is going to be a stunning vision that is a sign that in community, there is great power and healing. The extravagance in charity lies in the way it blesses giver and receiver. The blessing in the act of doing charity for one another is that love is poured out on us all. So many people are pouring their time and talent and treasures into this café that it feels like it is becoming holy ground.

Another group of more than twenty-five volunteers are

collecting the precious teacups, to use both as serving cups and as the principal interior design element. The group is tying them to strings, and making five chandeliers that will hang in the café, each a testament to how love that is poured out carries a deeper meaning that lasts well after the tea is gone. This café is teaching us all that holy ground comes from a community pouring out blessings and consecrating a space as sacred by words and deeds. Cemeteries are some of the holiest grounds in this world, places where people have been poured out and laid to rest. I saw the blossom of a huge thistle growing in a natural cemetery recently. Thistles have long been our symbol that a noxious weed that grows where the women we serve walk and sleep is filled with a beautiful purple center. The thistles are reminders to me that everything on God's green earth is beloved.

Near the cemetery there are ten-foot-tall thistle plants that still haven't bloomed. They are huge and stunning. I wanted to gather the whole community, hold hands, and sing our hearts out. I wanted us to sing because in the middle of even an old cemetery there is life, and it is powerful and stunning. These thistles have taproots that must reach down another ten feet. That means this plant, not yet fully grown, is over twenty feet high. The earth around it nurtures it. The plants' forbearers offered their seeds from wind and rain to take root. This is how I see the community of Thistle Farms right now: twenty feet high and growing taller from the trials of opening new businesses, launching a national conference at Thistle Farms and the café, and burying friends and family this year. Our community was planted on rich soil, and we have nothing to fear. Our community is standing twenty feet tall, and it is a sign of love's power and grace. I am holding all the women who still are on the streets and suffering in troubled fields from sexual violence, mental health, trauma, loneliness, and trafficking in my thoughts at the foot of this giant thistle.

Story and perseverance are part of what makes our thistle stand tall in the troubled fields of this world. With more gratitude and love than I have words for, I am a thistle farmer. I can imagine that this café, rooted as beautifully as this thistle and fed on the rich dirt of love in community, will be as big and stunning as thistles are. Later that same day I sat in a corner of the cemetery and drank a cup of green jasmine tea. It was as sweet and tender as the feelings that arose from seeing the thistle and glimpsing the powerful movement for women's freedom we are building. It is easy to feel the gratitude for the pouring out of spirit that gives us life, thistles, and tea.

One other sign of the spirit pouring out is tears. At Thistle Farms, a woman had taken part of her paycheck to buy eyelashes. She said the next day at work, she was so full of the spirit of love that she laughed and cried so much that one set of them fell off. She said she had no idea two years ago that she could feel this happy. It is remarkable when you think about her story. She was sexually abused for years. Her journey continued, like that of so many women all over our small globe, to spiral out of her control until she realized she was going in and out of jail and nothing was changing. She has made a journey from horrific trauma on just about every level to knowing joy so fully she laughs until her fake eyelashes fall off. That epitomizes healing. She drank it in and took hold in her core until it poured out. She is the preacher who reminds me that being poured out does not leave a person empty. It leaves a fragrance that fills a room. It leaves memory so full that it fills the teller with gratitude. It leaves places of new insight that are worth more than the tea ever was.

*Chapter Fourteen*

# THE HALOED LIGHT
# OF TEA

## Justice Tea

Caroline Logsdon, a dear friend of mine, tells the story of learning about justice tea from Thailand. The way to serve this tea is to let 2 tablespoons loose-leaf tea float freely in a teapot with water heated to 180 degrees. Filter it as you pour it through a strainer into a cup.

At a local restaurant in Chiang Mai in the northern area of Thailand, the cook prepared a pot of oolong tea for Caroline. She described in detail when she returned to Nashville how the leaves were grown in the mountains near Mae Salong, replacing the opium fields. The people who harvest at this elevation, including Thai, Chinese, Lisu, and Akha villagers, have a long history of resisting the communist rule in China and Burma. This tea is grown by a community with a sense that generations share the food, work, and gifts.

LIGHT SEEPS THROUGH THE smallest cracks like hope. There is a small town in Tennessee called Craggy Hope. The name itself sounds like a place with only a speck of hope poking through gray and lifeless rock. When you crest the hill in the town, the image is reinforced by the gray of exposed limestone cutting through the brown grass and three old buzzards sitting in a barren hackberry tree. There is a cabin by the road with a worn-out rebel flag hanging from the clothesline near a bunch of trash and old tires. Across the road is a fenced-in field with just one sheep standing there looking abandoned and alone.

I keep remembering that scene as I think about one of the women at Thistle Farms saying in an interview that she had begged a john to kill her, just so the pain would stop. She said, "I left him and living in hotels and walking around in a daze and so mad at myself and so confused and I couldn't even prostitute right. There were women walking by this old brown car where a man was trying to pick up a woman. I thought they were just passing up money. So I went in the car with him and, by the end of it, I was begging him to kill me. It was violent and painful and worse than I could imagine, and I left his car and went out again. I can't imagine, I was hurt and tired, but I kept walking." She was completely alone in this world.

It is in stories like hers, which are all too familiar and

horrid, that it's easy to find the strength to keep walking toward building the café. I keep thinking about that single sheep down in Craggy Hope—lonely and forsaken. I couldn't turn away from the sheep in Craggy Hope that day. It is closer to home than I want to admit. The places that epitomize our fear and make the hairs stick up on the backs of our necks are the ones to seek. Then we know the gift of the sliver of light. It is in the places where we are alone and lost that we appreciate light most of all.

That same kind of sliver of light can be found dancing in a fresh cup of brewed tea. A cup of oolong made with flower petals is the color of sunshine. With sunlight as bright as a noonday sun over a Nebraska field, the reflection is so clear I can distinguish the tones in my skin. The light from the cup reflects the sunlight as haloed rings dance inside the cup as the liquid searches for the lowest point. If you look into this single perfect cup of tea in just the right way, it appears as if the whole sun is sitting inside. Light has been dancing prominently in my head for weeks now. As spring breaks free, there is light everywhere. It is pouring into the café through the four huge new windows the contractors broke through the concrete walls. It is rising in the thousands of new wildflowers pushing through the hard winter ground. It is sitting on my lap as I write in the early morning by the kitchen window, and it is filling spaces with hope that have been darkened for weeks.

I noticed one of the more remarkable images of light I have ever seen early in the morning this spring. It was still dark as I awoke from sleeping on the floor in the San

Eduardo Chapel in Ecuador. As I waited for dawn, I saw a beautiful image of a stained glass window on the wall. I had never seen it before, even though I had been sleeping in this chapel for fifteen years during an annual retreat. The image was made from light coming from ventilation cutouts in the concrete wall in the shape of a flower, casting a rosette image on the opposite wall. The light was haloed as it moved and faded with the coming dawn in the middle of the world. What I felt lying there was how all light feels hallowed when we have hearts wide open in the midst of a concrete chapel off a dirt road. In moments such as these, when we remember we are on holy ground, no cathedral is more adorned. In such light, beauty rises from within as truth brushes past and carries us to hope. Light in teacups and dancing on walls become signs of God's light.

I wondered if something like a vision of light on stone had carried Mary Magdalene through the Easter morning events. The story of the Resurrection begins with the words "while it was still dark." The light has not yet risen on Jerusalem after the Sabbath as she heads out with grief as her guide to carry her to Jesus' body. And that is when light and shadow begin their dance like stained glass on concrete. A sliver of light is enough for her to see the stone in front of Jesus' tomb rolled away and to run toward Peter and John. As they run back to the tomb in a race with the murky light of dawn, they see enough to know Jesus is gone. Mary Magdalene stands alone and tries to see through tears and shadows. The light is surely breaking through as she sees angels and linen on the floor. Then, even as she cannot make out what she is seeing, she hears Jesus calling her. Then the true light of hope fills her from within, and she reaches for Jesus.

The week after I laid my sister's ashes inside the altar at the A-frame Chapel, I led a Eucharist with the same words and motions I have used every week for twenty years. As I lifted the round unleavened bread, I recited the last prayer: "And at the last day bring us with all your saints into the joy of your eternal kingdom." As I raised the host, there was a beautiful light with depth filling the center. I almost couldn't break it; I just stood there drawn into it. It had something to do with the silver paten, the lighting in the room, the angle I was holding the bread, and the space that grief opens in us. I wrote that night that I couldn't make out what the light was, maybe a lion, but even though it was unclear, I longed for it. The next Sunday, although the preacher and I had not talked with one another, he talked about a vision and said, "Imagine walking into church at night. The candles are the only source of light. Rest your eyes upon the host as it begins to send out rays of light that enter you and flood your soul, cleansing you. The rays soak into your body."

I asked the preacher where the image came from and if he saw a shape in the light. He said he just felt it. Even murky and shadowed light carries rays of hope in grief. Those rays are enough to bring all of us to a garden while it is still dark, ready to anoint a body, but hopeful enough when we see a sliver of light on rock or bread to run to find answers.

I kept thinking about the light in the host and shining on the wall after we left the chapel and traveled to the eight-hundred-year-old town of Cuenca, Ecuador. Early on the Sabbath, a group of us walked into the cathedral as communion was ending. We approached the altar as the remaining host was being placed in a tabernacle cross, and there it was. In the golden cross holding the host, the light I had glimpsed at the altar and that the preacher described was shining. It looked like a lion's mane. That light is always there; it is just that sometimes we have to walk through death and letting go to behold it.

When we let light flood our stone hearts, we can feel hope pouring into grief itself. All we grieve is full of light. In the right light, it is possible to feel the hope that danced the first morning of creation, that shines in the darkness, and that will lead us home. A sliver of light can cast stained glass on poor concrete walls, turn bread into a heavenly host, and cut through our darkness enough so we can see we are bathed in the light of love. It means that we can live in hope, dedicated to justice and truth, knowing the light will never leave us. That is the depth and beauty of the light that I see in my cup of tea. That is the kind of light that is ours for the beholding. This morning I celebrate all the light I have ever been graced to see and feel. I offer a toast to the source of all light before my next sip. I wish I could feel this light all the time.

But these days there are hardly enough hours in the day or time to sit and stare into a sweet cup of tea. Everyone on staff is working seven days a week, and we are running so fast that the real issue right now is losing focus and cutting out the light as we try to cut corners. This week the contractors told us the roof has a leak; we can't afford the sound system or signage; and we have to finalize decisions amid the vying tastes in the interior design and color. It is time to call the team together, bathe in the light of our mission, and see how we can reflect that light through the next weeks before we open. This is the time to stay in the light that has led us this far and not run in fear or get frustrated and live in the shadow parts of our hearts.

Every day there are volunteer groups priming the walls, tying teacups to light fixtures, cleaning wood, building a deck, and figuring out how to make menus from thistle paper. We knew from the beginning that having hundreds of volunteers help create this space would mean hundreds of loyal customers. The volunteer crews will be proud of the mission and want to purchase their tea and show their friends what they did in the name of justice. What I forgot is the burden that such huge numbers of volunteers put on staff members, who end up organizing most of the efforts. The quicker we add a bit to our coffers, make color and tile decisions, and simplify some of the design elements, the faster some of the stress and running around might subside. Part of leadership is not only holding people accountable to deadlines but knowing when to ease the load a bit to get to the goal.

We backed up the opening another week but now have a firm commitment from the mayor that he will cut the ribbon on the café on May 24. We are now officially beginning a countdown, and anything we can do to make it to the goal with our light and love still shining would be good. One of the best things I can think to do this morning is just keep looking into this beautiful cup of light green tea and offering a prayer. We all need to keep seeing the light and walking toward its peace.

Light and darkness travel hand and hand. Because of my work for the past couple of decades, I have ventured into places not lots of folks are privileged to see. Places like prisons, underneath bridges, and alleys that hold some of the worst secrets of all. Places where rays of light and moments of hope are particularly beautiful. All of it has been a huge gift and an exploration into the heart as well as the harder parts of this world. We just returned this week from driving out with a U-Haul on the back of a huge pickup truck to a prison in rural Tennessee where a group of men built cabinets for our café. This work came from a partnership with the Department of Corrections under the leadership of Tom Robinson, who felt that the men could support the women in their work toward independence and recovery. It was a beautiful act of restorative justice that was probably as beneficial for the men as the women. We promised the men that we would take pictures of the cabinets when the café opened so that they could see how their skills were being put to good use in our sanctuary.

It is no easy task getting a U-Haul trailer pulled by a big pickup in and out of a prison. The first issue is that prison officials don't like people driving huge trucks into prisons. We pulled up to the gate and even though our arrival was planned, three correctional officers in vehicles surrounded us. They explained that you are not allowed to pull up to the gate like that and asked us to back up. Courtney, the great project leader for the café, was driving, and we both looked at each other. Backing up with a big trailer is not easy, and this was the first time either of us had tried it. The correctional officer explained that you have to turn the wheel in the opposite direction you would like the trailer to go in. To me that felt like he said, "I am going to need you to spin around on your toes while we all make fun of you." So, they let Courtney and me step out of the truck and they took over. Unfortunately, the young man who took over was not an expert in backing up either, and as the taunts on the walkie-talkie increased, he was unable to get us out. Finally another guard helped, and we were able to load about $20,000 worth of cabinets gifted to us by talented incarcerated carpenters into our U-Haul and get back to the Thistle Stop Café.

When we got there to unload, I tried to get two construction guys to drink tea with me. They explained they didn't drink hot tea, ever. One man was a Seventh-day Adventist; the other, with a thick-drawled country accent, explained that he didn't drink anything after coffee in the morning except water until he got off work, when he switched to beer. That is just how he was, he said. I said please and told them I'd be really grateful if they would just stop for a minute before we had to unload all these cabinets and just sit and try one cup of our thistle blend with me, but I was flatly rejected.

I was a tea evangelist failure and felt that if I had said it differently or maybe was different, they might have said yes. I get all caught up and confused by rejection. It trips me up and makes me question my abilities and myself. I think what I see and feel should be clear to everyone and that if I just say it again, they will see my light. That is truly messed up! Moments like these are when we get ourselves in the way of the beautiful light shining around us and trip on our own shadows. There is an image in the Gospels of the disciples finding no acceptance in a town. Jesus gives them the first liturgical dance move (followed two chapters later by Lazarus's "resurrection hop" as he comes out of his tomb in a shroud) of kicking dust off shoes and walking with peace. Instead it's like I stand at a door letting the dust swirl up around my head as I knock and knock, begging someone to tell me I am good and what I believe is right. When the two men said no thanks, I should have just kicked up my heels and said, "Great, let's unload the cabinets," but instead it took another fifteen minutes for them to tell me about their religious backgrounds, potential addiction issues, and most of their family histories and tragedies. I am sure they were as exhausted by me as I was by myself.

People have a need for others to accept their ideas as their own. But that is not the calling of the Gospels or the calling of the way of tea. That way is simply to live and serve others and get out of our own way. We unloaded the cabinets and marveled that the men built them for us. This whole thing is a gift, and I need to unwrap it more gently.

In the midst of light, it is not hard to see the shadows and remember how many things are hidden by what we have yet to uncover in this work and on our journey. The mysterious dark interior hills of China that were opened after the Opium Wars seem like a space where lightness and darkness danced in huge tea gardens spread over hillsides. The early tea botanist and spy Robert Fortune made his way into places not everyone gets to travel to, to learn the secrets of tea. He marveled at the stunning beauty and light that only a handful of westerners had ever seen. He could not have imagined the angle of the light, the generosity of the people he feared, or the high esteem in which the farmers held the tea. Tea has always been about light and darkness. It calls us to praise the light and the way it shines on hillsides and forests. It calls us to see the slivers as potential for growth. The haloed light of tea calls us to explore the shadows and drink in the wonder that has shined in our hearts since the first dawn.

*Chapter Fifteen*

# THE LAST DROP

## Maté Tea

Maté is a tradition as well as a drink made from the Central American yerba plant. Maté is traditionally steeped and served in a hollow calabash gourd (itself called a maté) and drunk through a metal straw called a *bombilla* (pronounced bome-bee-ja). I use a regular teacup and the bombilla.

If you want to drink a traditional maté, the first thing to do is purchase a dried gourd. Then take it home and cure it by cutting off the stem and filling it with boiling water. After you let it sit for ten minutes, scrape the membrane out of the gourd under running water. Finally, put the cleaned-out gourd in the sunlight for a day or two until it is completely dry.

Pack the gourd about half full of dry yerba maté and turn the gourd upside down. Shake the more powdery leaves to the top of the gourd. This helps to ensure that you don't suck in the powdery leaves through the bombilla later. Slowly and carefully tilt the gourd right-side up so that the yerba maté remains in a lopsided pile on one side. Put the bombilla in the empty space next to the pile, then add cold water into the empty space until just before it reaches the top of the pile. Wait for it to be absorbed, and try to keep the powdery tip of the pile dry. Pour hot water into the empty space as you did with the cool water. Let it sit for a few minutes until you see that all the water has been absorbed by the yerba. This will make the yerba swell up and prevent your bombilla from plugging up. Cover the tip of the bombilla with your thumb and push it to the low spot in the bottom of the gourd. Then pour the rest of the hot water in and enjoy.

HOPE IS BEING POURED out like a whole pot of tea into a single cup. It is running over and giving us new energy to finish the project. The bouts of loneliness through the past eighteen months still haunt me, but even as I sit alone before the opening, humility and gratitude take center stage. This small community has given hope and new life to a once-forsaken space. We can taste the justice tea we will serve, smell the fresh bread we will offer, and imagine the new friends who will come through the doors with new stories. On the eve of the idea of a café coming into being, I am praying that our deepest dreams of loving the world land with a big splash. I remember when the first prayers for this project began. I think if we could see prayers when they are born, they might look light enough to attach themselves to a breath and float in the air like a hawk in an upward draft. Most new prayers must circle around our heads until gravity pulls them down to the ground, and there they are laid to rest. But other prayers float out beyond gravity. As they rise into the sky, they might look more like a kite tail that we are trying to keep flying in a fairly windless sky. But somehow they get high enough to wave in the wind and move toward the heavens. Floating freely, they aren't dragged down by reason or doubt. Eventually, like the kite tail, they become so small and distant that they are simply lost in the oblivion of space, swallowed up by the universe. They have no impact; they just disappear.

But every now and then a prayer born in that space between head and heart takes on dimension and weight. It doesn't move like a kite tail; it is more like a shooting star. It feels different. It has purpose and weight and pushes things out of the way to make room for itself. This mysterious prayer travels not into oblivion but in the fabric of creation. It sits with God, right in God's bosom, and has a place. This is the place of hither and yon where, every now and then, we can visit. It is not here or there; it isn't inside or outside our bodies. We can't really put a finger on it. It is a place we are privileged to see and to taste in small bites. Humanity was created to commune with this place, and we have been traveling there since original grace.

## My Journey

*I grew up in a family of addiction. My mother is an addict. My father is an addict. I lost three of my uncles and my sister to addiction. My uncle used to get high at my house all the time. I liked to watch the smoke swirl in the pipe but never tried it. One day my uncle offered me a hit. I took my first hit of crack cocaine with him and became very addicted. I was going to Medical Career College at the time. I was trying to smoke dope all night and still go to school. In the end, the drugs overcame my ambition to finish school, so I dropped out.*

*My addiction progressed. I had never tricked before, but my addiction led me to the streets. I prostituted to support my high. I started walking the streets and lost all respect for myself. My children even watched me walk the neighborhoods while they were outside playing. I was tired of selling my body for drugs. I was so tired and wanted to stop. One day I was sitting under a tree getting high and crying, when I began to pray and ask God to take this addiction from me. There was a church across the street from where I was sitting so I went into that church, sat on the back bench, and sincerely talked to the Lord. I asked Him to give me peace and joy in my life. He did! That was ten years ago, and I've been clean and sober ever since that day. I'm a 2005 gradu-ate. I'm grateful for a chance at life.*

—Terry Mitchell, Barista

It is miraculous to me to believe that our finite and fearful bodies can birth prayers of infinite proportions. It means we are eternal in our spirits and more than flesh and bone. It means we need to honor one another and make sure that space is sacred. It means I need to respect your prayers. It means when we worship, we are giving ourselves permission to imagine, dream, pray, and commune with God from a place within ourselves. As I sit alone holding a cup of tea, I imagine the scene at the café as the volun-teers put the finishing touches on it. Trees being planted by a friend and decorator. Formal touches like pillows for couches and purple ribbon for the mayor to cut.

All of the prayers that come to fruition do not sate our souls. Because they fill us with hope, new dreams start to arise. It is like tea. Even after a perfect cup, we still are thirsty the next day. If we sipped a cup that settled our souls, maybe we wouldn't feel the drive to keep striving for justice in women, tea, and life. If I lost my thirst for justice in the small things that I confront in my life, maybe I would lose the fire to fight against some of the biggest injustices the world faces.

My hope is that this café will be a sanctuary where we can bear our loneliness in community. That when we sip these cups of tea, we will believe that we are inching the world toward the side of justice like the oceans rise one drop of rain at a time.

It is time. It is time to open the café. The inspector came and pointed out the flaws in our construction, including the deck and the fire doors, about an hour and half before the mayor was coming and gave us a ninety-day permit so we can open and fix it as we go. The contemplation of the space between inspiration and action is memory. The vision has moved out of the way to make room for reality. "Ready or not, here we come" is the call to this dance. Grace is the music playing that spins us around and around until we feel dizzy with joy. It is a graceful thing to think a small thought and watch a beautiful community come together and make it into something bigger and more stunning than any of us could imagine alone. It's been hard sometimes with immeasurable stress on people like Courtney and Kathy. But my Lord, we did it. We have a stunning café with a hundred seats, a world-class sound system provided by Reba road manager Carolyn Snell, and lavender plants and trees surrounding a deck. Six chandeliers and eight hundred teacups, sleeves with our logo, and syrup to flavor coffee. The band is coming, and we are ready to welcome three hundred people through the door to see if we are as good as our word.

The grand opening was exactly that. Donors, well-wishers, the mayor and councilmen, judges and country music singers attended as well as John Seigenthaler, a civil rights hero here in Nashville. We spent nine hours meeting and greeting all the well-wishers. The café was filled with hope, and you could feel it like a breeze brushing against people's cheeks as they took in the beautiful floor, chandeliers, and countertops. All I wanted to do was thank everyone from the depths of my heart. The hope brought with it tremendous joy that took me by surprise. As community gathered, I could feel my heart rising in my chest. That joy was wondrous. I felt like I was seeing a stone rolled away or a surprise party.

The opening ceremony ended with my husband, Marcus, and son Levi singing their song, "Make It Love." Before he started singing, Levi leaned into the mike and said, "Mom, of all the things you have done, this is the coolest." Then they sang, "Take the pain that's been hanging around, take the rain that's been falling down, and let's just make it love. Take the hearts that are bound to break, and the burned-out stars so far away, and let's just make it love." To see them singing through the prism of welled-up tears made them look like a sparkling sea of love.

All the new residents of Magdalene came in a van to the opening. One had come directly from the streets of Nashville, and she greeted people saying "I'm a Magdalene woman; welcome." The other newest woman sat on the floor near the front and was literally washed in the light from the new windows. Her knees were crossed and she was just looking and listening to a couple of the thank-you speeches. When I stood by her, she got up and faced me. Studded ears, buzz-cropped hair, and sagging jeans were a harsh exterior to a heart as melted as my own. She started crying as she hugged me. Not just a few tears. I could feel her weeping into my chest as we both felt the bottom of our hearts, and I just held her. I can't imagine the ocean of tears between here and freedom for her. Tears for all she needs to forgive and be forgiven of. Tears for all the time she remembers trying to survive and all the time she has forgotten. Tears for the luck that has at least kept her alive and for now out of prison. Tears for the hardness reflected on the streets at night and the soft light she was soaking in. Tears for her family, her pain, the hope that didn't die, and the dreams she is imagining. God willing, she is done forever living on the streets. God willing, this café will be a huge success and will be hiring her in three months. God willing, she lets those tears run deep enough to be a river that runs toward justice and freedom.

I don't want to forget the details of the day. After I gave thanks for volunteers, board members, and staff, we all took turns at the mike thanking another fifty people. When there are truly more people to thank than you can list, you know the soil is rich enough to let scattered ideas take a root and produce a hundredfold. Seeing Jennifer, Anika, Terry, Arleatha, Christy, and Ronza in their purple aprons making tea in a French press with huge smiles was like looking into the kingdom. Courtney and Kathy had stayed until ten the night before the opening hanging the stories we had written, buying a clock, pulling out the stirrers and cup holders, and fixing a million other details where guests can feel the intention of the café as a welcoming sanctuary. There was a moment when I got to meet the very first two donors, Peggy Napier and Catherine Snell. As I began to thank them, I told them that this journey was a gift I will never forget. I thanked them both, holding my hands to my chest. Both were offering ideas of things we could sell, like tea cozies and gift certificates. As they stepped back into the crowd, I realized how limited language is in the expression of gratitude. I think the best way to show them and the hundred other volunteers and staff gratitude is to keep working toward the freedom of women. Both donors remarked about how their gift was part of their own healing and gratitude.

The gratitude I felt during the opening is simply one of the greatest feelings in the entire world. It leaves me with the desire to tell every young seminarian, "Just do the work of loving the world for days and days and years and years and feel how you are being pulled by a tide of thanksgiving into an ocean of gratitude that is bigger than anything you have ever known. It's not like having a gratitude list; it's being overcome by the lavish notion of gratitude itself. It's thinking, I'd do it all again to feel this. It's seeing everyone's eyes as beautiful and wondering how in God's name you are lucky enough to be in this space with all these people talking about love more than anything else. That changes a person's constitution as much as tea or charity or even prayer itself. I want to try every tea on the shelf in a different cup and bathe in the light some more and see what else rises as we welcome the community to come in. Our first day of operation is tomorrow and I pray, *God, please let people be thirsty, let the weather be unseasonably cold, and let the women remember everything they learned in barista training. Let the tip jar be full and the teapots poured out. Let the stories be honored, and keep everyone safe and loving toward one another. Finally, let this be the first day of years and years of us trying to love the whole world, one teacup at a time.*

As I started contemplating the next ventures for our band of sisters, I imagined planting a tea garden of our own. It would take years to grow and harvest, but we would know how the tea was cultivated and processed and could share our vision of justice tea with a wider world. We are not grandiose about opening a stunning café, we are grandiose about the possibilities that this small café and our new ventures can offer in the balance of love in the world. From this space women will be healed, people will be fed, and people from around the country will come and know they can help be a part of a revolution to change this world for women raped, trafficked, and addicted. This café helps us be a part of a living and breathing movement, and we will be better able to keep going now that we have this way of tea to help sustain us.

The time between inspiration and the reality of the waking dream was exactly what was required to gain the insight and momentum we needed, even though we were almost six months behind schedule. It was hard and stressful at times for everyone involved, including a committee with competing ideas, a shortage of funds, and the fact that none of us had opened a tea and coffee shop. But at the moment of birth, the grand opening, gratitude was so fierce that time and many mistakes were swept aside to make room for its grand presence. The first days of the business passed like a blur with a continuation of an outpouring of love. Just in the first couple of weeks, we had achieved our sales budget for the whole first month and actually had come in several thousand dollars under our expense budget. We were off and running, and now the work of the staff managing and making tea at the café would determine the success of the venture. By the time this book is published, thousands of cups of tea will have been poured. A thousand cups of tea served to others begins by looking into our own cups. In them, we can find the gift of contemplation that helps us see how to offer it to others. In our own cups of tea, we find the resolve and strength needed to do the work necessary to serve. And in our own cups of tea, we find the healing in our story can be a balm for others. We look into our own teacups first, so that we can serve them well to others.

I want to walk the way of tea and justice for the sake of people like my sister Katie and for my mother, who has been dead twenty years, and my father, who has been dead forty-five years. I want to walk the way with more intention and grace because of them. We all are graced with gifts as simple as *chado*, the way of tea, and as deep as love to carry us through days as bright and joyful as the café opening and as raw and hard as disappointment and grief. The way of tea and justice reminds us that we are heading toward healing. Nothing in this world can take away the glory of how the sun lights up the back of cloud just after sunset or lessen the beauty of a field of bluebells on a hillside in spring.

I led a funeral right after the opening of the café and then went straight to a small tea party that had already been scheduled to celebrate the opening. I didn't know how that would work, but it felt congruous and like grief and ritual love each other. Rituals for grieving and celebrating walk hand in hand and keep us upright and moving forward. The end is dramatic, simply because it becomes the last—whether it is the ending of a cup of tea, the ending of a book, or the ending of a life. Knowing it is the end makes the moments that sometimes go by unnoticed have heft and spiritual depth. What if this is our last cup of tea or the last words I write? It is good to remember that there will be an ending to this sweet tea party.

If we knew which cup would be our last, we would sip it differently and taste it with all that we are. If this were my last cup, I would remember all the people who shared tea with me over these last few years. I would think about friends who traveled all over the globe and were willing to share stories with me about the meaning of the tea. I would think back on the first time I peered into a teacup and tried to read the leaves and remember how one can interpret signs in life a million ways. Then I would thank God I saw hope in my reading. If it were my last cup, I am sure I would weep and grieve all the cups of tea I will never drink with the people I love so much. I would remember my mom using every tea bag twice to save money and the tea set my children gave me for Christmas last year. Thanksgivings over our last cups of tea make them so sweet we need to salt them with tears that rise in us when we think of saying good-bye to the way of tea and life.

And so to end this treatise on tea and justice, I end with a toast of tea to love. This toast is raised to the heavens in honor of tea drinkers who have found the way of tea and justice to be the path that leads us to love itself. In the end, if love is not the last word on tea and justice, we missed the point of the tea journey anyway.

# THE TEA PARTY

*A pot of tea is shared in old Cairo*
*By wise men who knew the old Pharaoh.*
*They set a fine table beside the road*
*The trinity of Jesus, Muhammad, and Moses.*

*Tired of witnessing the countless hordes*
*That turned holy books into swords.*
*Tired of death in their collective name*
*They sip their tea and bear the shame.*

*For the sake of love they have surrendered talk*
*Choosing chado and silent walks.*
*They call the faithful to do the same*
*And offer tea in love's holy name.*

*Toasting they refill their cups*
*"To the holy one that fills us up."*
*No defense of truth is needed*
*When for love's sake they have all ceded.*

—Becca Stevens

*Peggy Napier*

*Before construction began*

*Peggy Napier*

*After café opened June 2013*

When we consider how small after all the cup of human enjoyment is, how soon overflowed with tears, how easily drained to the dregs in our quenchless thirst for infinity, we shall not blame ourselves for making so much of the tea-cup.

—Kakuzo Okakura, *The Book of Tea*

# Notes

*A Brief Introduction to the World of Tea*

1 Cheryl Sternman Rule, "Types of Tea," *Culinate,*
last modified October 6, 2008, accessed April 10,
2014, http://www.culinate.com/articles/culinate8/
tea_leaves.

*Chapter 1: Reading Tea Leaves*

2 Andrea Israel and Pamela Mitchell, *Taking Tea: The
Essential Guide to Brewing, Serving, and Entertaining
with Teas from around the World* (New York:
Weidenfeld & Nicolson, 1987), 80.

*Chapter 2: Dreaming a Cup of Tea*

3 Roy Moxham, A Brief History of Tea (Philadelphia:
Running Press, 2009), 18.
4 Ibid., 176.
5 Ibid.
6 Victor H. Mair and Erling Hoh, *The True History of
Tea* (New York: Thames & Hudson, 2009), 244.
7 As evidenced in the 2008 Danish documentary *The
Bitter Taste of Tea,* directed by Tom Heinemann and
produced by Erling Borgen and Tom Heinemann.

8 The Benedictine rule is the disciplined way the
monastic community formed in the fifth century
lived out their spiritual practice.

## Chapter 3: Drinking Tea in Community

9 Julian of Norwich. *Revelations of Divine Love*, trans.
Elizabeth Spearing (Penguin Classics, 1998), chapter
LXXII, 175.

10 Moxham, *The Brief History of Tea*, 30–40.

11 As Oliver Goldsmith wrote, "What a jovial and merry
world would this be, may it please your worships, but
for that inextricable labyrinth of debts, cares, woe,
wants, grief, discontent, melancholy, large jointure,
impositions and lies." Oliver Goldsmith, "Letter XVII,"
*The Citizen of the World. 1760–1761. The Norton
Anthology of English Literature: The 18th Century.*
Accessed April 10, 2014, https://www.wwnorton.com/
college/english/nael/18century/topic_4/goldsmith.htm.

12 Tea was described then as "an exotic luxury...a favorite
way among the upper classes to signify civility and
taste in the chilly, wet climate of Britain. From there
it rapidly percolated downward through society so that
by the mid-eighteenth century tea had become the
most popular drink throughout Britain, outselling even
beer." Sarah Rose, *For All the Tea in China: How
England Stole the World's Favorite Drink and Changed
History* (New York: Penguin, 2011), 25.

The East India Company was founded in 1600 and
then claimed a monopoly on tea for more than two

centuries. The trouble with the trading practices of Britain was that they started with growing poppies in India that were turned into balls of opium. The opium was shipped to China and traded for tea. "The tea being drunk in the West—at Methodist and antislavery meetings, in fine drawing rooms and poor cottages—nearly all of it was bought with opium." James Norwood Pratt, "Trading Tea for Opium," *TeaMuse*, last modified May 2001, accessed April 10, 2014, http://www.teamuse.com/article_010502.html.

## Chapter 6: Aromatic Sweet Cups

13 Marion Cabell Tyree, *Housekeeping in Old Virginia* (Louisville, KY: John P. Morton & Co., 1878).

## Chapter 7: The Paradise of Tea

14 Teresa of Avila, *Interior Castle*, trans. and ed. E. Allison Peers (New York: Image Books, 1961).

15 Victor H. Mair and Erling Hoh, *The True History of Tea* (New York: Thames & Hudson, 2009), 242.

16 Grahame, Kenneth. *The Wind in the Willows* (New York: Sterling Children's Books, 2005), 105.

## Chapter 9: A Cup of Understanding

17 Kakuzo Okakura, *The Book of Tea* (New York: Dover, 1964), 145.

## Chapter 11: Tea Resolutions

18 "New Year's," *History.com*, Accessed April 10, 2014, http://www.history.com/topics/holidays/new-years.

*Notes*

**Chapter 12: Tea Retreats**

19 James N. Pratt, *The Ultimate Tea Lover's Treasury* (San Francisco: Tea Society, 2011), 14.

**Chapter 13: Pouring Out**

20 George Orwell, *The Collected Essays, Journalism and Letters of George Orwell, Vol. 3*, ed. Sonia Orwell and Ian Angus (New York: Harcourt, Brace, and World, 1968), 42.

# Bibliography

*The Bitter Taste of Tea*. Dir. Tom Heinemann. Prod. Erling Borgen and Tom Heinemann. 2008. Documentary. Denmark.

Duriez, Colin. *Tolkien and C. S. Lewis: The Gift of Friendship*. Mahwah, NJ: HiddenSpring, 2003.

Fong, Roy. *The Great Teas of China*. Oakland, CA: Tea Journey, 2007.

Gschwendner, Albert. *Book of Tea*, 6th ed. Meckenheim, Germany: TeaGschwendner, 2009.

Heiss, Mary Lou, and Robert J. Heiss. *The Story of Tea: A Cultural History and Drinking Guide*. Berkeley, CA: Ten Speed, 2007.

Israel, Andrea, and Pamela Mitchell. *Taking Tea: The Essential Guide to Brewing, Serving, and Entertaining with Teas from around the World*. New York: Weidenfeld & Nicolson, 1987.

Mair, Victor H., and Erling Hoh. *The True History of Tea*. New York: Thames & Hudson, 2009.

Moxham, Roy. *A Brief History of Tea*. Philadelphia: Running Press, 2009.

Okakura, Kakuzo. *The Book of Tea*. New York: Dover, 1964. Originally published in 1906.

Okakura, Tenshin. *Cha No Hon: Eibunban.* Tokyo: Kodansha Intanashonaru, 2005.

Pratt, James Norwood. *James Norwood Pratt's Tea Dictionary.* Los Angeles: Tea Society, 2010.

Pratt, James N. *The Ultimate Tea Lover's Treasury.* San Francisco: Tea Society, 2011.

Rose, Sarah. *For All the Tea in China: How England Stole the World's Favorite Drink and Changed History.* New York: Penguin, 2011.